TAL Russell
Sept. '82

BARNUM

A Musical
Suggested by the
life of P.T. Barnum

BARNUM

By
Mark Bramble
Lyrics by
Michael Stewart

Nelson Doubleday, Inc.
Garden City, New York

Manufactured in the United States of America

Design by Jeanette Portelli
Photographs by Martha Swope

Barnum opened at Broadway's St. James Theatre on April 30, 1980. It was directed and staged by Joe Layton, and produced by Judy Gordon, Cy Coleman, Maurice & Lois F. Rosenfield in association with Irvin Feld and Kenneth Feld. Scenery was designed by David Mitchell; costumes by Theoni V. Aldredge; lighting by Craig Miller; and sound by Otis Munderloh. The music director was Peter Howard, with vocal arrangements by Cy Coleman and Jeremy Stone, and orchestrations by Hershy Kay. The cast was as follows:

PHINEAS TAYLOR BARNUM	*Jim Dale*
CHAIRY BARNUM	*Catherine Cox*
RINGMASTER	*Terrence V. Mann*
CHESTER LYMAN	*R. J. Lewis*
JOICE HETH	*Lillias White*
AMOS SCUDDER	*Kelly Walters*
LADY PLATE BALANCER	*Catherine Carr*
LADY JUGGLER	*Barbara Nadel*
BATON TWIRLER	*Darlene Cory*
CHIEF BRICKLAYER	*Fred Garbo Garver*
WHITE-FACED CLOWN	*Andy Teirstein*
SHERWOOD STRATTON	*R. J. Lewis*
MRS. SHERWOOD STRATTON	*Barbara Nadel*
TOM THUMB	*Leonard John Crofoot*
SUSAN B. ANTHONY	*Karen Trott*
JULIUS GOLDSCHMIDT	*Terrence V. Mann*
JENNY LIND	*Marianne Tatum*
ONE-MAN BAND	*Steven Michael Harris*
WILTON	*Bruce Robertson*
EDGAR TEMPLETON	*Kelly Walters*
HUMBERT MORRISSEY	*R. J. Lewis*
LADY AERIALIST	*Robbi Morgan*
JAMES A. BAILEY	*Terrence V. Mann*

BARNUM

The Evening

Commencing one-half hour before the show
Barker Outside Theatre

With tours through The Exhibition of Wonders
in the lobbies

And Diversions in the theatre by
Members of the Company

Characters

PHINEAS TAYLOR BARNUM
CHARITY BARNUM
RINGMASTER
CHESTER LYMAN
JOICE HETH
AMOS SCUDDER
TWO WAITRESSES
WHITE-FACED CLOWN
SHERWOOD STRATTON
MRS. SHERWOOD STRATTON
TOM THUMB
JULIUS GOLDSCHMIDT
JENNY LIND
ONE-MAN BAND
WILTON
EDGAR TEMPLETON
HUMBERT MORRISSEY
JAMES A. BAILEY

And

Clowns, Bricklayers, Acrobats, Tumblers, Gymnasts, Jugglers, The Bridgeport Pageant Choir, Bands of Every Size, Shape, and Description, the Mob in general, and Characters too numerous to mention.

Time: 1835 through 1880
The action takes place all over America
and the major capitals of the world

The Musical Numbers

ACT I

"There Is A Sucker Born Ev'ry Minute"	*Barnum*
"Thank God I'm Old"	*Joice Heth and Tambourine Players*
"The Colors Of My Life"	*Barnum, then Chairy*
"One Brick At A Time"	*Chairy, Barnum and Bricklayers*
"Museum Song"	*Barnum*
"I Like Your Style"	*Barnum and Chairy*
"Bigger Isn't Better"	*Tom Thumb*
"Love Makes Such Fools Of Us All"	*Jenny Lind*
"Out There"	*Barnum*

ACT II

"Come Follow The Band"	*The Potomac Marching Band and Washingtonians*
"Black And White"	*Chairy, Choir, Blues Singer, Barnum, Citizens of Bridgeport*
"The Colors Of My Life" (Reprise)	*Barnum and Chairy*
"The Prince Of Humbug"	*Barnum*
"Join The Circus"	*James A. Bailey, All Circus Performers and Barnum*

Prologue

(*As in the circus, the show begins a half hour before the curtain goes up. On the sidewalk under the theatre marquee a bunting-festooned platform is set out and a young Barker in period costume steps onto the tiny stage.*)

BARKER: (*Over calliope music*) . . . Step right up, ladies and gentlemen, and welcome to *Barnum!* The doors will be opening in a few minutes and Mr. Barnum has asked me to extend a particular welcome to you this evening, and to the very first performance of *Barnum* here at the beautiful St. James Theatre. For those of you who have not yet secured your places for this educational and uplifting entertainment, our box-office staff under the courteous direction of Mr. Medford Brady is waiting to serve you at both windows to my right—I believe there are a few choice locations still remaining—and for those ladies and gentlemen already holding tickets, the doors will be opening shortly. In the meanwhile, may I draw your attention to this cane . . . (*And Barker performs first set of sidewalk illusions ending with applause, as he continues*) Ladies and gentlemen, the doors seem to be opening and for those of you already holding tickets, I would like to draw your attention to a comprehensive Exhibition of Wonders featuring life-sized illustrations of some of Mr. Barnum's most renowned attractions that is being held in the inner lobby before the performance begins. Under the guidance of Miss Amy Beecher you will hear about such international wonders as Ann Swann, the world's tallest woman—Chang and Eng, the authentic Siamese Twins—Grizzly Adams and his famed California Animal Menagerie—and many, many more. This thrilling exhibition which alone is worth twice the price of admission, is available only to ticket holders so if you have not already secured these precious commodities, I urge you to do so at once. And now—while those fortunate patrons are waiting for their escorts to complete their negotiations with the esteemed Mr. Brady, I'd like to show you this coin . . . (*Barker performs coin tricks with audience, ending in applause, as he continues*) . . . I assume by now that all present have acquired their tickets—if not, Mr. Brady is still waiting to serve you at either window inside. For those of you still in attendance, I have an interesting and unusual demonstration . . . (*And he performs a series of magic tricks and illusions, ending in applause, as he continues*) And now, ladies and gentlemen, I urge you to hurry, the performance will begin in fifteen minutes and I don't want you to miss the Exhibition of Wonders in the inner lobby . . . Right this way . . . Through both doors . . .

(*Barker suddenly turns, starting over for a new group of patrons. At the same time Barker is delivering his spiel outside the theatre Miss Amy Beecher, a young woman in period costume, conducts guided tours through the Exhibition of Wonders in the inner lobby and smoking lounge. The Exhibition consists of arts and artifacts relating to many of Barnum's most famous attractions, beginning as Miss Beecher announces . . .*)

MISS AMY BEECHER: . . . Good evening, ladies and gentlemen, and welcome to the Exhibition of Wonders—a collection of arts and artifacts depicting the struggles and triumphs of Phineas Taylor Barnum's illustrious career. Surely there are those in American history who stand for higher achievement in literature, science, and art—but there is none more typical of genuine American enterprise, indomitable will, unfailing courage, and unerring instinct for success. (*Indicating etching with pointer*) This etching shows the great showman's humble birthplace in Bethel, Connecticut, about one hundred miles north of New York City, where Mr. Barnum was born in 1810. Like so many of his famous compatriots, Mr. Barnum came of good old New England Heritage. His ancestors were among the settlers of Massachusetts and Connecticut. (*Moving on to next position, indicating Joice Heth handbill*) . . . Ladies and gentlemen, this handbill dates from 1835 when Mr. Barnum presented his first attraction—Joice Heth, the Oldest Woman Alive. Mr. Barnum purchased the contract to present Joice Heth for one thousand dollars and exhibited her in New York City, Boston, Philadelphia, Pittsburgh, and many other places where his halls were thronged. (*Continued, as she indicates various prints, posters, photos, etc.*) Here is Mr. Barnum's famed American Museum in New York City which he opened New Year's Day, 1842. The American Museum was the World's Largest, Grandest, Best amusement institution and held 600,000 exhibitions including Educated Fleas—Albinos—Gerta the Fat Girl, over five hundred pounds—a Tribe of Aborigines—Ann Swann, the world's tallest woman—Chang and Eng, the authentic Siamese Twins—Grizzly Adams and his famed California Animal Menagerie—Niagara Falls with Real Water—Living Statuary—Glass Blowing—Indian War Dances—Stuffed and Live Gorillas—every sight, wonder, and phenomenon known to mankind. (*Indicating pictures relating to burning of the American Museum*) . . . On July 13, 1865, due to a gas leak, Barnum's American Museum burned to the ground destroying 600,000 exhibitions. (*Indicating pic-*

ture) Here is Mr. Barnum himself as proprietor of the museum. (*Moving on to Tom Thumb display*) . . . None of Barnum's attractions has been more famous than Tom Thumb, the smallest man in the world, twenty-five inches from toe to crown! Tom Thumb made his debut on December 8, 1842, in the good city of Philadelphia. (*Holding it up*) This is an actual ticket to one of Tom Thumb's entertainments at London's famed Egyptian Hall. Of the eighty-two million tickets sold for P. T. Barnum's attractions, *twenty million* were sold by Tom Thumb alone. (*Indicating picture of Tom Thumb's wedding*) . . . On February 21, 1873, Tom Thumb married Lavinia Warren, a lady who was just a few inches shorter than he was. (*Turning to case with chair*) In the case to my left is Tom Thumb's favorite chair. Half his house was regular size for receiving visitors and half was scaled down for the comfort of Mr. and Mrs. Thumb. (*Moving on to Jenny Lind section*) . . . In September 1850, Barnum engaged Jenny Lind, the Swedish Nightingale, for one hundred concerts in the United States. This painting shows Jenny Lind's arrival in New York. Eight months earlier no one in America had known who she was, but with Barnum's gentle prodding thirty thousand were on hand to greet her ship. (*Indicating program*) To my left a program from Jenny Lind's first American concert at Castle Garden in New York City on the evening of September 11, 1850. She was paid an unprecedented fee of one thousand dollars for each concert as well as a percentage of the house. (*Moving on to Jumbo section*) . . . Jumbo the Children's Giant Pet, brought to America by Mr. Barnum from the Royal Zoological Society of London. Jumbo measured twelve feet tall at the shoulder and weighed six and one-half tons. With his seven-foot trunk, he was capable of reaching an object twenty-six feet from the ground. His diet included two hundred pounds of hay and a quart of Bourbon whiskey each day. (*Turning to the magnificent display for Barnum and Bailey's Greatest*

Show on Earth, she continues) . . . Mr. Barnum retired from the exhibition and menagerie business for several years of active public and business life, returning to entertainment in 1880 when he joined forces with Mr. James A. Bailey to create the Greatest Show on Earth. To my right you will find a collection of posters and photographs showing Barnum and Bailey's most renowned attractions available for your viewing pleasure before you take your seats.

(*And she crosses back to first picture and starts tour over again. During this entire period various members of the company perform divertissements throughout the auditorium for arriving patrons, including magic tricks, balloon sculptures, mime acts—whatever you want* . . .)

Act I

(*Curtain is up as audience comes into theatre revealing a tent-like structure soaring high above a single circus ring extending out over the orchestra pit. Before house lights start down, man with trap drum and musician with concertina come on and play tiny fanfare as man in shirtsleeves strides out on stage*)

MAN IN SHIRTSLEEVES: . . . Barnum's the name, P. T. Barnum, and I want to tell you that tonight, on this stage, you are going to see—bar none—every sight, wonder, and miracle that name stands for! (*Continuing excitedly as company starts quietly out Right and Left*) Including Jumbo, the Largest Elephant in the World; the Amazing Great White Whale from Labrador; General Tom Thumb, only twenty-five inches from toe to crown; Joice Heth, the Oldest Woman Alive; the Rarest and Most Beautiful Bird in Captivity, the Swedish Nightingale; plus a Company of Hundreds—no, Thousands—including Marching Bands, Standing Bands, Tumbling Bands, Flying Bands, Bands of Every Size, Shape, and Description . . . and here they are! (*As company bows*) . . . Oh, I know what you're thinking, you don't see any Nightingales or Flying Bands or Twenty-five-inch Men—but like I told you Barnum's my name and miracles are my game—and they're all up there, mark my word! (*Suddenly to woman in Stage Right Box, as she gets up*) Wait a minute! Where are you going?

WOMAN IN BOX: Home.

BARNUM: But I got a point of view to expound, defending the noble art of Humbug.

WOMAN IN BOX: (*As she puts knitting in bag*) Which I happen to be in disagreement with as it is no more than a shoddy defense of flim-flam, so it doesn't behoove me to stick around.

BARNUM: Respect for the speaker, Madam, requires you to listen while he sets forth his convictions!

WOMAN IN BOX: And respect for my own convictions requires me to set forth, which I am doing.

BARNUM: Then go! Isolated dissent is hardly going to deter me! One small voice can quite easily be ignored!

WOMAN IN BOX: Good day, Mr. Barnum.

BARNUM: Course it doesn't help any if that one small voice belongs to his wife. (*To woman in box*) . . . Chairy Barnum, I'll have a kiss before you leave.

WOMAN IN BOX: With pleasure, Mr. Barnum.

(*Barnum hurries Right, jumps from trampoline into box and kisses her*)

BARNUM: . . . You may not make much sense . . . but you're beautiful.

RINGMASTER: (*Stepping onto platform high above Stage Left Box as through this musicians start out*) In the Main Ring, ladies and gentlemen, the fight-to-the finish struggle of Humbug versus Truth, Flim-Flam versus Fact, Mr. Phineas Taylor Barnum versus his good wife, Charity, an American Pageant featuring Stirring Music, Thrilling Spectacle, Hilarious Clowns, and Savage Jungle Beasts! (*As he slides down rope to stage*) . . . Presenting first Mr. Barnum himself in an opening bit of Philosophic Folderol. Mr. Barnum!

BARNUM: Fact is, my wife's a perfect example of what I'm talkin' about. Give her a mess of hard facts and she's happy as a clam, serve her up a bit of fancy and she turns up her nose like it was yesterday's fish. But whether you end up thinking humbug's a blessing or a curse, you're *still* gonna buy it! Why? Because every sixty seconds in this world a delightful phenomenon takes place which absolutely guarantees it. (*And he sings*)

THERE IS A SUCKER
BORN EV'RY MINUTE
EACH TIME THAT SECOND HAND SWEEPS TO THE TOP
LIKE DANDELIONS UP THEY POP
THEIR EARS SO BIG, THEIR EYES SO WIDE
AND THOUGH I FEED 'EM BONAFIDE
BALONEY
WITH NO TRUTH IN IT
WHY YOU CAN BET I'LL FIND SOME RUBE TO BUY MY CORN
'CAUSE THERE'S A SURE-AS-SHOOTIN' SUCKER BORN A MINUTE
AND I'M REFERRIN' TO
THE MINUTE YOU
WAS BORN.

EACH BLESSED HOUR
BRINGS SIXTY OF 'EM

EACH TIME THAT WOODEN CUCKOO SHOWS HIS FACE
ANOTHER SUCKER TAKES HIS PLACE
AND PLUNKS HIS QUARTER ON THE LINE
TO BUY MY BRAND OF GENUINE
MULARKEY
GOD BLESS AND LOVE 'EM
BUT DON'T FEEL SAD OR HOPPIN' MAD OR CAUSE A SCENE
'CAUSE THERE'S A SURE-AS-SHOOTIN' SUCKER BORN A MINUTE
BUT MA'AM YOU MIGHTA BEEN
THE MINUTE IN
BETWEEN.

IF I ALLOW THAT RIGHT HERE IN MY HAND'S
THE SMALLEST LIVIN' HUMAN MAN
THE SIGHT OF THAT IS SURELY WORTH A DIME.
IF I PRESENT AN EDUCATED POOCH
WHO'S TRAINED TO DANCE THE HOOCHY-KOOCH
WHAT BETTER WAY TO WASTE A BIT OF TIME?
IF I IMPORT AT MONUMENTAL COST
A LADY FAIR WHOSE HEAD WAS LOST
WHILE CROSSIN' RAILROAD TRACKS TO PICK SOME ZINNIAS
WHO EATS FARINA THROUGH A HOSE
AND WEARS PINK TIGHTS INSTEAD OF CLOTHES
IF THAT AIN'T WORTH A BUCK MY NAME AIN'T PHINEAS!
YOU SAY THAT'S HOGWASH, WELL WHO CARES
YOU'LL BUY MY HOGWASH LONG AS THERE'S . . .

A SUCKER
BORN EV'RY MINUTE
EACH TIME THE SECOND HAND SWEEPS TO THE TOP
LIKE DANDELIONS UP THEY POP
THEIR EARS SO BIG THEIR EYES SO WIDE
AND THOUGH MY TALE IS BONAFIDE
BALONEY
JUST LET ME SPIN IT
AND AIN'T NO MAN WHO CAN RESIST ME, WAIT AND SEE
'CAUSE THERE'S A SURE-AS-SHOOTIN' SUCKER BORN A MINUTE

AND FRIENDS, THE BIGGEST ONE
EXCLUDIN' NONE
IS ME!

(*End song, applause, then as music fades, Barnum continues*)

COURSE THAT WAS WHEN OUR COUNTRY WAS A PUP.
TODAY, ALAS, IT'S GROWIN' UP
AND WE AIN'T GOT NO SUCKERS ANYMORE . . .

(*As music continues*)

. . . I'll prove it to you! If I was to tell you I got a real live mermaid back there, how many would pay twenty-five cents to see her? Maybe one. Two at the most. The rest of you so educated you don't believe any foolishness like a half-woman, half-fish. So you're not suckers. (*As Wally pulls on Mermaid Booth Left*) And you're missing a helluva lot because there happens to be one behind that curtain, but now I'll be damned if I'll show her to you! I don't think she's et yet, Wally, so would you ask her to put on that middy blouse I got for her, I don't want you getting all wrought up when you open the wine. (*Suddenly to house as Booth goes off*) . . . Sit down you! Oh, now you're interested! When you hear Mademoiselle Neptuna's got no blouse on that gets you up on your feet! Well, it happens to be the mystic joining of earth and ocean that's the miracle, sir, not her uncovered bosoms . . . (*With a chuckle*) Pearly pink and simply beautiful though they may be!

CHAIRY: (*Coming on Right*) . . . Here it is in Mr. Webster's dictionary, Taylor. Humbug—"Something designed to deceive or mislead."

BARNUM: (*To us*) That's what comes of marrying a schoolteacher, they go right to the books! (*Back to her*) . . .

Chairy, I'm talking about rosy possibilities! The kind of humbug that bunch of Pilgrims sold themselves when they set sail on the *Mayflower*. The dream, Chairy!

CHAIRY: Just one question, Taylor. That lady eating farina with no head; how does she chew the lumps?

BARNUM: Well now, Chairy, she's got herself this small boy who . . .

CHAIRY: Mr. Webster gives this nice synonym for humbug too. Lies. (*Kissing him, then starting off*) . . . Now don't give up, Taylor. The evening's young. You've still got some rosy possibilities.

(*Circus chase music as Ringmaster starts out Left on tall unicycle carrying lasso*)

RINGMASTER: (*Blowing whistle*) . . . In the Far Ring, Humble Beginnings, as Mr. Phineas Taylor Barnum, in his first appearance in the Main Tent, turns Old into Gold quicker than you can say—George Washington!

(*Ringmaster throws lasso off Right and backs off pulling on wagon containing Chester Lyman, a shifty-eyed gentleman, and Joice Heth, a black lady, sitting at battered upright as we find ourselves in front of Niblo's Gardens, New York, 1835*)

LYMAN: . . . I'm telling you they came by the thousands in Philadelphia, Mr. Barnum! (*Handing papers to Barnum*) Now here's all the papers you'll need. Birth certificate, bill of sale, writs and testimony proving beyond the shadow of a doubt that on June fifteenth Joice Heth will be one hundred and sixty years old!

BARNUM: She'd better be, Mr. Lyman. It's taken every cent I have to buy this contract, but from now on P. T. Barnum presents . . . (*Painting billboard on air*) . . . "Joice Heth, the Oldest Woman in the World!"

LYMAN: (*Snatching cash from Barnum*) She'll make your fortune, Mr. Barnum. (*As he exits*) . . . Just remember Philadelphia!

BARNUM: All right, Joice, we better get to work if we want to eat tonight. (*To passersby as Joice plays*) . . . Step right up and see her—Joice Heth, the Oldest Woman in the World!

JOICE HETH: (*Singing lackadaisically as Barnum barks the attraction,* "Step right up, ladies and gentlemen, only ten cents to see Joice Heth, the Oldest Woman in the World!")

WHEN YOU SEE THE SHAPE THE WORLD IS IN
WHEN THE WAY IT IS AIN'T WHAT IT'S BEEN
WHEN FOLKS JUST CARE FOR GOLD
THANK GOD I'M OLD!
WHEN YOU TAKE A GANDER AT THE NEWS
WHEN YOU HEAR THE LANGUAGE PEOPLE USE
WHEN NO SWEET SONGS ARE SUNG
I DON'T WANNA BE YOUNG
WHEN YOU SEE THE WAY FOLKS MISBEHAVE . . .

BARNUM: (*Cutting her off*) . . . I don't understand it. They came by the thousands in Philadelphia!

JOICE HETH: And walked by, by the thousands. You been had, Mista Barnum. (*She spits*) . . . Anyway, what's so special about an old lady? A young lady, that's different. If you had me up here a hunnerd and forty years ago they woulda' come all right . . .

BARNUM: What'd you say?

JOICE HETH: I says what's so special 'bout an old lady?

BARNUM: But a special old lady . . .

JOICE HETH: (*As he stares at her*) Mista Barnum, whut you lookin' at?

BARNUM: I'm looking at a nurse about a hundred years ago, you got this baby bouncing on your knee . . . (*An idea hits*) . . . George Washington!

JOICE HETH: (*Shaking her head*) I don't know no people named Washin'ton.

BARNUM: George Washington, the Father of Our Country.

JOICE HETH: I told you I don't know any . . .

BARNUM: Joice, that sidewalk looks a mite hard to sleep on and I'd say there was a fair chance of rain tonight. Maybe even hail . . .

JOICE HETH: What'd you say that boy's name was?

BARNUM: *George Washington!*

JOICE HETH: (*Seeing the light*) You means lil' Georgie? Why, Mista Barnum, I pretty near raised that boy!

BARNUM: (*As he puts up sign reading "Joice Heth, Nurse to George Washington" and Joice begins playing*) All right, Joice, let's do it! (*To passersby*) . . . Step right up and see her—Joice Heth, George Washington's Nurse!

JOICE HETH: (*Singing, as through the following passersby begin gathering*)

WHEN YOU SEE THE SHAPE THE WORLD IS IN
WHEN THE WAY IT IS AIN'T WHAT IT'S BEEN
WHEN FOLKS JUST CARE FOR GOLD
THANK GOD I'M OLD!
WHEN YOU TAKE A GANDER AT THE NEWS
WHEN YOU HEAR THE LANGUAGE PEOPLE USE
WHEN NO SWEET SONGS ARE SUNG
I DON'T WANNA BE YOUNG

BARNUM: (*As he takes her chair*) . . . You got 'em, Joice, now liven it up!

JOICE HETH:

DADDY TIME HE
DOESN'T FRET ME
SHOULD HE SPY ME
THAT DON'T UPSET ME
LET HIM EYE ME
COME AND GET ME
THAT'S FINE BY ME
AGE DON'T WORRY ME . . .

BARNUM: . . . One hundred and sixty years old!

JOICE HETH:

WHEN YOU SEE THE WAY FOLKS MISBEHAVE
WHEN IT'S ONLY GOOD TIMES THAT THEY CRAVE
WHEN KIDS ARE MUCH TOO BOLD
THANK GOD I'M OLD!
WHEN THERE AIN'T NO HE-MEN LEFT ALIVE
WHEN THEY TELL YOU THREE MEN OUT OF FIVE
END UP LOCKED UP OR HUNG
I DON'T WANNA BE YOUNG

BARNUM: (*As Joice continues playing*) . . . Do some steps for them, Joice!

JOICE HETH: I'm a hunnerd and sixty years old, I can't dance.

BARNUM: Rain, hail, and maybe a blizzard, Joice!

JOICE HETH: I'll dance. (*And she climbs off wagon and attempts a dance as Barnum barks* "One-hundred-and-sixty-year-old legs!" *At a certain point in dance, Joice says . . .*)

JOICE HETH: . . . Lemme tell you 'bout the day Georgie discovered America!

BARNUM: That was Christopher Columbus.

JOICE HETH: I tended him too. (*By now she is completely carried away and continues dance joined by Barnum and tambourinists. End dance and she sings*)

GONNA GET ME DRESSED AND POWDERED DOWN
CALL MYSELF A HACK AND GO TO TOWN
SEE EV'RY SHADY STREET
THESE FEET ONCE STROLLED
THEN I'M GONNA SLIP BACK ON THE SHELF
HAVE A LITTLE NIP AND TELL MYSELF
THOUGH MY BACK BUCKLES AND BENDS
MY HAIR GOT SILVERY ENDS
WHEN I SEE ALL OF MY FRIENDS
LAID OUT AND COLD . . .
THANK GOD I'M OLD!

BARNUM: (*Stepping out of group after applause as others push Joice and wagon off*) . . . All right, maybe I misled 'em a bit, but those folks went home thinking they shook the hand that held the rosy bottom of the father of this country, and that's a patriotic humbug and there's none better! (*Crossing to door Down Left*) Now that Joice was a success I started signing up other attractions—and I needed some place to put 'em! (*And he opens door as Amos Scudder steps out*)

AMOS SCUDDER: . . . That's right, Mr. Barnum, I'm lookin' for a partner to run the American Museum, but I don't want to turn it into no sideshow.

BARNUM: I couldn't agree with you more, Mr. Scudder, that's why I intend filling all five floors with the most educational attractions imaginable including three galleries of art, a lecture hall seating two thousand people, and in the rotunda a glass tank containing a living, breathing, spouting Great White Whale from Labrador! (*Quickly handing him ticket before Scudder can speak*) . . . And just to help you make up your mind may I present you with this courtesy ticket entitling you and a friend to two free admissions upon payment of one-half the regular price any Tuesday, Wednesday, or Thursday between the hours of twelve noon and one P.M., is it a deal?

CHAIRY: (*Coming angrily on Left, slamming door*) Taylor Barnum, did you or did you not have an appointment to take me to lunch at one o'clock sharp? It is now *past* two-fourteen!

RINGMASTER: (*As tumbler comes out, cracks whip*) . . . In the Near Ring, ladies and gentlemen, Mr. P. T. Barnum faces that most Ferocious of all Jungle Beasts—the Female of the Species who has been kept waiting over one hour and fourteen minutes! (*As he starts off*) Mr. Barnum will face this Dangerous Creature unarmed!

(*Barnum starts toward Chairy, then suddenly turns to Scudder*)

BARNUM: Darn it, Mr. Scudder, I thought I asked you to tell me when it was one o'clock! (*Before Scudder can an-*

swer) . . . No excuses, just run along and I'll meet you and the builders at the Museum at two forty-five. (*As Scudder exits with a* "Very well, Mr. Barnum") Chairy, I don't know why I ever took him as a partner, he's so forgetful! (*To us*) . . . A perfect example of a marital humbug. Trouble is, with my wife it never works.

CHAIRY: Hogwash, Taylor. I believe you forgot that appointment all by yourself. (*As Barnum looks at us and says,* "You see?") . . . Now, I have to pick up some pamphlets over at the Women's Emporium, so I thought we might lunch there.

BARNUM: Chairy, you can't get *lunch* in that place, but McNally's Oyster House is right round the corner so I suggest . . .

CHAIRY: That we leave it up to the Fates. An excellent idea. (*Taking coin from her purse*) . . . Heads the Women's Emporium, tails McNally's.

BARNUM: I'll toss it if you don't mind.

CHAIRY: Go right ahead, Taylor. I trust you one hundred percent.

(*He takes coin, rubs it, spits on it, tosses it in the air, then slaps it on back of his wrist. He slowly uncovers it and shrugs in defeat as plate balancers, girls juggling cutlery, and tumblers with table and chairs come on while sign reading, "The Women's Emporium—Where Women Work for Equal Wages," drops in as two well-scrubbed young women come on from Left*)

FIRST WOMAN: (*Excitedly, handing Chairy pamphlet*) . . . Here it is, Mrs. Barnum, our new pamphlet, all about the

Stanton Act. Thanks to Elizabeth Cady Stanton, the State of New York now guarantees a woman the right to make all her own business and legal decisions!

SECOND WOMAN: What do you think of that, Mr. Barnum?

BARNUM: I'm all for it. A hundred percent. As long as she asks her husband first! All right, McNally, bring us a couple of dozen oysters and two large ales—and put a head on 'em!

CHAIRY: (*Hastily*) Mr. Barnum will have the liver special, Mrs. Mortimer, plus fresh boiled parsnips . . . (*Before Barnum can speak*) . . . And an extra copy of Miss Stanton's pamphlet for dessert. (*As Barnum shakes head "no" and waitresses start off Left*) Now, Taylor, you can tell me who this new partner of yours is.

BARNUM: (*Taking a deep breath*) Chairy, that was Mr. Amos Scudder, him and me are rebuilding the American Museum.

CHAIRY: With what? We haven't a hundred dollars to our name.

BARNUM: Brass and a bit of humbug, you'd be surprised how often it's just as good as silver or gold . . .

CHAIRY: (*Shaking her head*) Schemes again, Taylor. Schemes and dreams.

BARNUM: That's my nature, Chairy! I told you I was a dreamer the first night I met you.

CHAIRY: Taylor Barnum, when a girl meets a man in the middle of the worst thunderstorm of the summer, with bolts of lightnin' jumpin' off every tree and barn in sight, and thunder so loud it nearly scares you out of your wits, not to mention the dogs and cats all over the territory howling to raise the dead, she don't pay much mind when a man happens to mention that he's a dreamer. (*Taking his hand*) . . . And I'm not sayin' you shouldn't have dreams, Taylor. Just let them be sensible ones we can reach.

BARNUM: Chairy, I want to excite people, stir 'em up, give 'em a glimpse of the miracle!

CHAIRY: Miracle's a pretty fancy word for humbug, Taylor.

BARNUM: How can you say that, Chairy? Maybe I put a high polish on the facts sometimes, but I've never taken anybody for one thin dime!

CHAIRY: You've taken them for more than money! You get them all wrought up about things that can never be like a woman a hundred and sixty years old. I don't mind you using the imagination the good Lord gave you, but with two daughters to bring up, you ought to be using it for more sensible things! (*As Barnum sighs, he's heard all this before*) . . . Now I happen to know Mr. Chauncy Jerome's looking for a partner over at the clock factory. I could be a part of it, Taylor, write the letters, keep the accounts . . .

BARNUM: Chairy, I just can't do it! Tick-tock-tick from ten to six every day with only an occasional bong to break the monotony of ten thousand cuckoos lookin' out of ten thousand little holes! Every man's got a temperament, Mrs. Barnum, and mine's just not suited to tick-tock, cuckoo, and bong.

CHAIRY: (*A bit hurt*) I'm sorry, Taylor. I shouldn't have brought it up.

BARNUM: Of course you should, Chairy! That's half a wife's job, bringing up things her husband doesn't want to hear. (*Tenderly, as music comes up*) . . . Chairy, a clock factory's just not the right *color* for me. Just say the name, Bridgeport Clockworks, and what do you see? Gray and brown and maybe if you're lucky a little dash of taupe. But walk inside any sideshow and you got fire-engine red and buttercup yellow and Kelly green and it's like livin' inside a giant pinwheel! And it's not just for my own selfish pleasure that I need all them colors, Chairy! (*As he pulls tablecloth out from under plates, cutlery, glassware, revealing a bright yellow cloth underneath*) . . . I want to splash 'em out for everybody in this whole world to see! (*And he sings. Through course of song, he illustrates his ideas by turning a decanter of water bright purple, changing a gray napkin to crimson, and finally spreading a rose-red wash across the entire cyclorama*)

THE COLORS OF MY LIFE
ARE BOUNTIFUL AND BOLD
THE PURPLE GLOW OF INDIGO
THE GLEAM OF GREEN AND GOLD
THE SPLENDOR OF A SUNRISE
THE DAZZLE OF A FLAME
THE GLORY OF A RAINBOW
I'D PUT 'EM ALL TO SHAME
NO QUIET BROWNS AND GRAYS
I'LL TAKE MY DAYS INSTEAD
AND FILL THEM TILL THEY OVERFLOW
WITH ROSE AND CHERRY RED!
AND SHOULD THIS SUNLIT WORLD GROW DARK ONE DAY
THE COLORS OF MY LIFE
WILL LEAVE A SHINING LIGHT
TO SHOW THE WAY . . .

CHAIRY: (*As music continues*) . . . That's well and good, Mr. Barnum, but your greens and reds aren't going to be much help if you don't get those builders started.

BARNUM: Good Lord, it's two-forty. Now, Chairy, you wait right here and I'll be back in five minutes, maybe ten, a half hour at the most—look, if I'm not back by six, come over to the Museum. Ann Street and Broadway. You'll know it by the sign—the red one, with purple trim and gold letters—that says Barnum's American Museum! (*And he sings*)

THE SPLENDOR OF A SUNRISE

(*As he pulls ball of flame from his hat*)

THE DAZZLE OF A FLAME

(*As he goes off Right*)

THE GLORY OF A RAINBOW
I'D PUT 'EM ALL TO SHAME . . .

CHAIRY: (*When he is gone, as music continues*) . . . It's your own fault, Charity Barnum! If you'd asked a few logical questions before you married him you would have put a healthy distance between yourself and a fella who wants to give the whole world a paint job! Which I'm not so sure it needs! (*And she sings*)

THE COLORS OF MY LIFE
ARE SOFTER THAN A BREEZE
THE SILVER-GRAY OF EIDERDOWN
THE DAPPLED GREEN OF TREES
THE AMBER OF A WHEATFIELD
THE HAZEL OF A SEED
THE CRYSTAL OF A RAINDROP
ARE ALL I'LL EVER NEED
YOUR REDS ARE MUCH TOO BOLD
IN GOLD I FIND NO WORTH
I'LL FILL MY DAYS WITH SAGE AND BROWN
THE COLORS OF THE EARTH
AND IF FROM BY MY SIDE MY LOVE SHOULD ROAM

THE COLORS OF MY LIFE
WILL SHINE A QUIET LIGHT
TO LEAD HIM HOME.

(*And she exits as Ringmaster appears Up Center on "walking ladder," tumbles to ground, and says*)

RINGMASTER: (*As Barnum and Amos Scudder enter Right and clown bricklayers start on from all directions*) . . . For Children of All Ages, a Cascade, a Caravan, a Cornucopia, a Cavalcade—of Cataclysmically Comical Clowns!

(*And Barnum, Amos Scudder, and bricklayers build a structure of sorts which comes tumbling down just as the keystone is put into place*)

BARNUM: (*Frantically, to Chairy who comes on at that point*) . . . Chairy, I bit off more than I can chew!

CHAIRY: (*As through this she takes off gloves, rolls up sleeves*) Nonsense.

BARNUM: We got an opening Monday morning at nine!

CHAIRY: We'll be ready.

BARNUM: Do you propose rebuilding an entire museum from top to bottom in two days?

CHAIRY: I do, my treasure.

BARNUM: But how, my dove?

CHAIRY: Slowly. (*And she sings*)

THE LORD GAVE EACH AND EV'RY ONE
THE SPUNK TO DO WHAT CAN'T BE DONE

THE BRAWN, THE BRAIN, THE COURAGE, AND THE HEART
THE STRENGTH TO BEND THE STRONGEST BAR
THE WILL TO REACH THE FARTHEST STAR
IT'S JUST A CASE OF LEARNING HOW TO START . . .

TO BUILD A TOW'R
UP SO HIGH
TO A CLOUD
YOU'LL ANCHOR
BUILD IT ONE TINY BRICK AT A TIME

BUCKS
MULTIPLY
TILL A BUM'S
A BANKER
JUST BEGIN WITH A THIN SILVER DIME

THAT EMPTY FIELD
IT CAN YIELD
MILES AND MILES OF FLOWERS
YOU DON'T NEED NO MAGIC POWERS
JUST A SEED
AND SHOWERS

FROM THE FLOOR
TO THE SKIES
YOU CAN SOAR
IF YOU'RE WISE ENOUGH TO CLIMB
ONE BRICK AT A TIME!

(The bricklayers have begun their task again, and now the Museum rises as they sing with Chairy, whose lines are in italics)

BRICKLAYERS/CHAIRY: *(Variously, as Barnum exits)*

TO BUILD A SHIP THAT'S BUILT TO LAST
You lay the keel, then raise the mast

AN ODE BEGINS WITH JUST A SIMPLE RHYME
AN OAK WITH ROOTS A MILE BENEATH
Becomes a stick to pick your teeth
JUST SHARPEN UP YOUR KNIFE AND TAKE YOUR TIME!

ONE STALWART CHAP
WITH A CUP
AND A BUNCH
OF HOURS
HE CAN SCOOP ALL THE SALT FROM THE SEA

BUDS
OPEN UP
TURNING BOWS
TO BOWERS
ALL BEGUN BY JUST ONE BUMBLE BEE

TO WRITE WITH EASE
SYMPHONIES
OR AT LEAST CANTATI
FILLED WITH TRILLS AND OBLIGATI
START WITH FA
SOL LA TI

LEAVE THE REST
IN THE DUST
BE THE BEST
IF YOU'RE JUST CONTENT TO CLIMB
ONE BRICK AT A TIME!

(Barnum and Amos Scudder exit Left as Chairy and bricklayers continue)

CHAIRY/BRICKLAYERS:

JUST TAKE
A BRICK

AND PLACE IT ON THE GROUND
TO MAKE IT STICK
POUR MORTAR ALL AROUND

A CUP
OF LIME
THEN STIR UNTIL IT'S HARD
AND UP
SHE'LL CLIMB
BY INCH, BY FOOT, BY YARD

A SILL
A DOOR
A LEDGE, A WINDOWPANE
THEN DRILL
SOME MORE
RAISE UP A WEATHER VANE

A ROOF
THE PROOF
THAT GOIN' SLOW LIKE THIS
A SPLENDID EDIFICE CAN CLIMB

(*Bricklayers form line throwing bricks from one to the next as Museum begins to take shape and they sing*)

BRICKLAYERS:

TO BUILD A TOW'R
UP SO HIGH
TO A CLOUD

YOU'LL ANCHOR
BUILD IT ONE TINY BRICK
AT A TIME

BUCKS
MULTIPLY

CHAIRY:

JUST TAKE
A BRICK
AND PLACE IT ON THE
GROUND
TO MAKE
IT STICK
POUR MORTAR ALL AROUND

A CUP
OF LIME

TILL A BUM'S
A BANKER
JUST BEGIN WITH A THIN
SILVER DIME

THAT EMPTY FIELD
IT CAN YIELD
MILES AND MILES OF
FLOWERS
YOU DON'T NEED NO MAGIC
POWERS
JUST A SEED
AND SHOWERS

FROM THE FLOOR
TO THE SKIES
YOU CAN SOAR
IF YOU'RE WISE ENOUGH TO
CLIMB
ONE BRICK AT A

THEN STIR UNTIL IT'S HARD
AND UP
SHE'LL CLIMB
BY INCH, BY FOOT, BY YARD

A SILL
A DOOR
A LEDGE, A WINDOWPANE

THEN DRILL

SOME MORE
RAISE UP A WEATHER VANE

A ROOF
THE PROOF
THAT GOIN' SLOW LIKE THIS
A SPLENDID EDIFICE CAN
CLIMB
ONE BRICK AT A

CHAIRY/BRICKLAYERS: (*Continued, as through course of this Barnum and Amos Scudder re-enter*)

ONE BRICK AT A TIME,
ONE SINGLE SOLITARY BRICK!
ONE BRICK AT A TIME,
ONE SINGLE SOLITARY BRICK!
ONE BRICK AT A TIME,
ONE SINGLE SOLITARY BRICK!
OOH, AAH, EEE, OH!
ONE BRICK AT A TIME!

(*Number ends as completed Museum is in place and patrons hold up dollar bills for admission*)

BARNUM: (*To us*) . . . Everything about my museum was spectacular, including the price. One dollar! Now that may seem a bit steep, but it was worth it. Look at what I gave 'em! (*And with banjo accompaniment, he sings*)

QUITE A LOTTA
ROMAN TERRA COTTA
LIVIN' LAVA FROM THE FLANKS OF ETNA
STATUARY
RIDE A DROMEDARY
SEE THE TEMPLE TUMBLE AND THE RED SEA PART

MACNAMARA'S BAND
THE FATTEST LADY IN THE LAND
A PICKLED PRE-HISTORIC HAND
A STRAND OF POCAHONTAS' HAIR
CROW AND SIOUX
WHO'RE GOIN' TO
BE SHOWIN' YOU
SOME ROWIN' THROUGH
A MODEL OF THE RAPIDS ON THE DELAWARE!

ARMADILLOS
STUFFED AND LIVE GORILLAS
REPRODUCTIONS OF THE CYCLOPS' RET'NA
CRYSTAL BLOWIN'
AUTOMATIC SEWIN'
VENUS ON A SHELL AND OTHER WORKS OF ART

EDUCATED FLEAS
A TRIBE OF ABORIGINES
TWO LADIES JOINED ACROSS THE KNEES
THE MONA LISA MADE OF ICE
HOTTENTOTS
WE'VE GOTTEN IN
FORGOTTEN SPOTS
A COTTON GIN
A NIGHT WITH LOT IN SODOM, BETTER SEE THAT TWICE!

ONE IGUANA
SNAKES AND OTHER FAUNA
GOT NO BEARDED LADY, BUT WE'RE GET'NA
WHEN YOU DUCK OUT
TAKE ANOTHER BUCK OUT
RUN AROUND THE BLOCK AND SEE A
RUN AROUND THE BLOCK AND SEE A
RUN AROUND THE BLOCK AND SEE A NEW SHOW START!

(*End song, applause, as Amos Scudder hurries on Left carrying ledger of receipts*)

AMOS SCUDDER: . . . Mr. Barnum! Mr. Barnum! Five thousand admissions! In one day! Only everybody's going downstairs to see the whale then upstairs to see the Indians and Joice Heth and the mermaid then back downstairs to start all over again! Nobody's going out, Mr. Barnum, what are we going to do?

BARNUM: (*As through this two egress columns enter Right and Left*) Put that sign I had printed over the back door —"To the Egress."

AMOS SCUDDER: "To the Egress"?

BARNUM: Don't get frightened, it's just a fancy word for exit.

AMOS SCUDDER: But no one will know what it means!

BARNUM: They will when they get outside. (*To us*) . . . That's a health and education humbug. They learn a new word and get some fresh air.

(*Music up as crowd starts to door saying variously,* "What's an Egress? It's a bird, I think, related to the stork. No matter what it is, Martha, I wanna see it!" *as Barnum sings*)

EDUCATED FLEAS
A TRIBE OF ABORIGINES
TWO LADIES JOINED ACROSS THE KNEES
THE MONA LISA MADE OF ICE
HOTTENTOTS
WE'VE GOTTEN IN
FORGOTTEN SPOTS
A COTTON GIN
A NIGHT WITH LOT IN SODOM, BETTER SEE THAT TWICE!

ONE IGUANA
SNAKES AND OTHER FAUNA
GOT NO BEARDED LADY, BUT WE'RE GET'NA
WHEN YOU DUCK OUT
TAKE ANOTHER BUCK OUT
RUN AROUND THE BLOCK AND SEE A
RUN AROUND THE BLOCK AND SEE A
RUN AROUND THE BLOCK AND SEE A NEW SHOW START!

(*Suddenly door starts to move away. Crowd follows it and one by one they pass through it and exit. Barnum is last one to join them and as he steps through it we find ourselves in back yard of Barnum home in Bridgeport as Chairy hangs laundry on clothesline*)

BARNUM: . . . Now I don't want you to turn 'round till I'm ready.

(*Circus chase music as door exits and Ringmaster comes out*)

RINGMASTER: (*As girl with parasol starts across wire*) Mr. P. T. Barnum, the Grand Master of the High Wire, tries for a triple somersault . . . (*She falls.*) . . . And falls! Which gets him plenty burned up.

(*Ringmaster and girl exit as Barnum says*)

BARNUM: All right—now.

CHAIRY: (*Opening eyes as he lifts string of pearls from box*) Good Lord they're real, what's the man done.

BARNUM: A foolish thing, Chairy! Married a hard-headed, cold-eyed, tough-talking New England lady . . . (*Tenderly, as musicians with mandolin and harmonica assemble under tree and begin playing softly through the following*) . . . Who's kept my crazy world from going up in smoke for fourteen years. Happy anniversary.

CHAIRY: I might've been foolish enough to marry you, Taylor, but that doesn't mean I can't count and our anniversary isn't for six months.

BARNUM: I'm talking about the museum, Chairy! Or did you forget we opened our doors to the public exactly one year ago today? Now put on your silks and satins, woman, because I intend taking you, me, and those pearls to celebrate tonight at Rector's Restaurant in New York City!

CHAIRY: I am sorry, Mr. Barnum, but I am not going to any Rector's Restaurant! The food's too rich, the people too fancy, and I don't want to even discuss the prices! I'm staying right here.

BARNUM: (*To us*) Marital Humbug Number Two—the carrot and club principle. It never fails. (*To Chairy*) . . . Now see here, Chairy, I've got the prettiest wife in the state of Connecticut and it's my God-given right to show her off if I want to! And if you don't go upstairs and change into your best dress *at once*, then certain very costly anniversary gifts might have to be returned. (*Chairy has taken off pearls through this, now hands them to him*) It *almost* never fails. (*Exasperatedly*) . . . Charity Barnum, what'm I gonna do with you?

CHAIRY: (*As music comes up*) Put up with me, Taylor. Same's I do with you.

(*And he sings, joined by Chairy, whose lyrics are in italics*)

BARNUM:

WE'RE OUT OF STEP
WE DISAGREE
WHAT'S RIGHT FOR YOU
IS WRONG FOR ME

BARNUM/CHAIRY:

TOGETHER WE'RE APART A COUNTRY MILE
BUT I LIKE YOUR STYLE!
I LIKE YOUR STYLE.
We're out of step
We disagree
What's right for you
Is wrong for me

When I propose
Then you protest
What's my delight
You just detest
Too sweet a fight to ever reconcile
TOO SWEET A FIGHT TO EVER RECONCILE
'Cause I like your style!
I LIKE YOUR STYLE
I like your style
I LIKE YOUR STYLE

No shouts or quarrels
No blows or tears

(*Unison*)

One simple fuss
To dissect and discuss
For the next one hundred years!

Each blessed day
We sweetly fill
With "No you won't"
And "Yes I will"
YOU WONDER HOW WE MADE IT DOWN THE AISLE
You wonder how we made it down the aisle
WELL I LIKED YOUR STYLE!
I like your style

(Music continues as Barnum and Chairy do an affectionate dance, then sing)

Each blessed day
EACH BLESSED DAY
We sweetly fill
WE SWEETLY FILL
With "No you won't"
WITH "NO YOU WON'T"
And "Yes I will"
AND "YES I WILL"
You wonder how we made it down the aisle
WONDER HOW WE MADE IT DOWN THE AISLE
Well I liked your style!
I LIKED YOUR STYLE!
I liked your style!
I LIKED YOUR STYLE!
I like your style
I liked your style!
STYLE, STYLE, STYLE!

(End song, applause, then as music continues Chairy starts off)

CHAIRY: . . . All right, Taylor, I'll change my dress. But it isn't to show off these pearls in front of your fancy New York friends! (*As she exits*) It's because I'm still in love with you, you great fool, and I want one of your damn marital humbugs to succeed.

BARNUM: (*Calling after her as Amos Scudder starts on from Right*) Chairy, I have *never* tried to humbug you! Why, I'm shocked at you even suggesting such a thing . . .

AMOS SCUDDER: Mr. Barnum?

BARNUM: Not now, Scudder, can't you see I'm lying to my wife. (*Realizing*) . . . What the devil brings you out here this time of night anyhow? (*Beginning to be alarmed*) Speak up, Mr. Scudder! Is anything wrong?

AMOS SCUDDER: A fire, Mr. Barnum. At the Museum . . . (*Barnum starts for door*) . . . No use going down there, there's nothing left. I'm sorry, Mr. Barnum.

BARNUM: (*As Scudder starts off, wanting it to be so*) . . . Mr. Scudder, I *hope* I'm being humbugged!

AMOS SCUDDER: (*Softly*) Alas, Mr. Barnum, you never taught me how.

BARNUM: (*Calling after him as he goes*) Mr. Scudder!

(*And Chairy—in her best dress—hurries excitedly back on*)

CHAIRY: . . . Now, Taylor, I'll tell you right now I don't intend dancing any gallops, I haven't had time to change my petticoat and it's the same old muslin one, but since the only dance you know's the waltz I don't anticipate any . . . (*Slowing down as she realizes something is wrong*) Problems.

BARNUM: Evening's off, Chairy. No use celebrating the anniversary of a museum . . . what's burned down. (*Before she can speak*) . . . And maybe that's a good thing! You were right, the darn place was nothing but a sideshow anyhow.

CHAIRY: Taylor Barnum, that museum was absolutely splendid—for what it was—and I will not listen to anything to the contrary! New York's not the only place to make a living, you know. There's a whole country out there! Why, right here in Bridgeport you could . . .

BARNUM: Darn it, Chairy, if you haven't come through with the solution! There *is* a whole country out there! Here I am piddling my life away corner of Broadway and Ann Street when there's two dozen states never even heard of P. T. Barnum! I'll build a new museum and put it on wheels!

CHAIRY: Taylor, I wasn't thinking about any two dozen states, Mr. Jerome's clockworks is . . .

BARNUM: Bring a little red and gold to the entire country! We can start with a three-month swing round the East, all I need's a bit of capital and one headline attraction to pull 'em in! And because it was your idea . . . (*As Chairy angrily says,* "What!" *he continues*) . . . I'm putting a top line on every ad, "Entire tour under the personal direction of Mr. and Mrs. P. T. Barnum!" (*Chairy is silent*) You *are* with me in this, aren't you, Chairy? (*We see her struggle*) . . . Chairy?

CHAIRY: Well, I'm not sure I'm one hundred percent in accord, Taylor . . .

BARNUM: Then everything's all right—we're quarreling again.

(*Music comes up as he takes her in his arms and they dance. A moment, then man comes on from Left*)

SHERWOOD STRATTON: . . . I hope I'm not interrupting, Mr. Barnum.

BARNUM: (*As they continue dancing*) You are, Mr. Stratton.

SHERWOOD STRATTON: But our appointment was for two o'clock.

BARNUM: (*Still dancing*) I'm busy now, we'll discuss it first thing Monday.

SHERWOOD STRATTON: (*Starting Left*) Why don't we forget it, my wife and I have a few moral qualms about your offer anyway.

BARNUM: Tomorrow morning at nine!

SHERWOOD STRATTON: Good day, Mr. Barnum.

BARNUM: All right, dammit, here I come. (*As he releases Chairy*) . . . Can't help it, Chairy—he's got that headline attraction I was telling you about! You go on dancing and I'll be back in two shakes.

(*Sad-faced clown bows to Chairy, puts out his arms and begins dancing her off as circus chase music comes up and three jugglers start on from Right to Left as Ringmaster enters Left*)

RINGMASTER: And now, a deliciously Droll Divertissement, as Mr. P. T. Barnum juggles Three Slippery Strattons—in the air!

BARNUM: All right, Stratton, what's this about "moral qualms"?

"Join the circus
Like you wanted to
When you were a kid
Climb aboard
Before it moves on and you'll
Thank your lucky stars you did..."

"We're out of step
We disagree
What's right for you
Is wrong for me
Together we're apart
A country mile
But I like your style!
I like your style."

Out there, somewhere, just out of sight
There's a world that's blazing with light
Ain't each man alive got the right
To stray just a mite from the straight and narrow
Shoot through the night like a flaming arrow."

"There is a sucker
Born ev'ry minute
Each time that second hand sweeps to the top
Like dandelions up they pop
Their ears so big, their eyes so wide
And though I feed 'em bona fide
Baloney
With no truth in it
Why you can bet I'll find some rube to buy my corn
'Cause there's a sure-as-shootin' sucker born a minute
And I'm referrin' to
The minute you
Was born."

Photographs by Martha Swope

STRATTON: (*As Mrs. Stratton joins him and we find ourselves in sitting room of Stratton home*) Let me begin by telling you that my wife and I have the highest regard for you.

BARNUM: (*To us*) I smell a humbug.

MRS. STRATTON: But as God is our witness . . .

BARNUM: (*Still to us*) A holy humbug, the worst kind.

MRS. STRATTON: But to permit you to exploit our son Charles's oddities for such a small sum of money is an offense to a Christian conscience.

BARNUM: (*To us*) Now the key word in that speech isn't Christian, it's *small.* As in sum of money. (*To Strattons*) . . . Now exactly what do you mean when you refer to oddities?

STRATTON: Any boy only twenty-five inches tall from head to toe is a freak of nature . . .

BARNUM: Hold on, Mr. Stratton. Joice Heth is a hundred and sixty years of age, Madame Josepha has a ten-inch beard, Ann Swann is eight and a half feet tall—but that doesn't make them freaks, it makes them *special!* (*Strattons start to interrupt*) . . . What you call an aberration of nature, I call a gift from God to lift him above the crowd! (*Overriding them again*) Tell you what, since he's old enough to make up his own mind, why don't we leave it up to the boy. (*Crossing to tiny armchair*) . . . Charley, I want you to come with me and join my show but I'm not gonna fool you. Tens, thousands, maybe millions of people are gonna come to see you—some to stare, maybe even a few to laugh—but most'll cheer and tell their children and grandchildren for generations to come that they saw the smallest man in the world. We'll even find you a special name—something to go with the miracle of your size—Thumb! Tom Thumb! Course, you also gotta keep in mind the princely salary to you and your dear family of fifteen dollars a week! Well, Charley, I've put it as fairly as I can . . . Now it's up to you.

(*A moment, then a tiny hand pops up from behind chair and signals "O.K."*)

BARNUM: (*Continued, to us, as Strattons exit Left*) What'd I say that name was? Thumb. Tom Thumb. Sounds a little skimpy to me, what we need is a handle to go with it . . . Sir Thomas Thumb! (*Dismissing it*) . . . The Right Honorable Tom Thumb! (*Rejecting that too*) Something with a touch of the military . . . Captain Tom Thumb. Oh, what the deuce, in for a penny, in for a pound . . . General Tom Thumb!

(*Strattons and Barnum have gone off through this as set begins to change. Before our eyes the armchair begins to grow in size until it is enormous. As this happens, we hear announcer's voice boom out*)

RINGMASTER'S VOICE: . . . Ladies and gentlemen of the great city of Philadelphia! For the first time anywhere . . . The world's smallest man . . . General Tom Thumb!

(*And Tom Thumb, in general's uniform, steps out from behind chair.* NOTE: THIS IS THE FIRST TIME WE SEE TOM THUMB. HE IS PLAYED BY A NORMAL-SIZED PERSON WITH EVERYTHING ON THE SET GIANT-SIZED TO CREATE THE ILLUSION THAT HE IS ONLY TWENTY-FIVE INCHES TALL)

TOM THUMB: (*Sings*)

I'M GEN'RAL THUMB JUST COME TO TOWN
A YANKEE DOODLE DANDY

I'VE ET YOUR SCRAPPLE, WASHED IT DOWN
WITH JUST A NIP OF BRANDY
THE MAYOR MADE ME PRESENTS RARE
THE LADIES DID SALUTE ME
FIRST RATE I AM THEY ALL DECLARE
AND ALL MY POSES SUIT ME!
MY SUCCESS SHOULD OPEN UP YOUR EYES
DON'T JUDGE NOTHING JUST BY SHAPE OR SIZE . . .

(*As he dances*)

BIGGER ISN'T BETTER
TALLER ISN'T BRAVER
STRONGER ISN'T ALWAYS WISE
SMALLER ISN'T NECES-
SARILY THE LESSER
GUTS CAN COME IN ANY SIZE
LADY LUCK CAN FAVOR
JUST A LITTLE SHAVER
OVER ONE WHO'S SIX-FOOT-THREE
BRAINS IN ANY TUSSLE
MOPS THE FLOOR WITH MUSCLE
BET YOUR LIFE I'M GLAD I'M ME!

RINGMASTER'S VOICE: (*Over music as two giant Beefeaters start on Left*) . . . Ladies and gentlemen, General Tom Thumb's engagement at London's Egyptian Hall has been canceled this evening due to his command performance at Buckingham Palace!

TOM THUMB:

BIGGER ISN'T KEENER
LARGER ISN'T BOLDER
HIGHER MIGHT BE LOW INSIDE
WHEN YOU NEED TO LEAN UP-
ON A FRIENDLY SHOULDER

NARROW'S JUST AS GOOD AS WIDE
SEE THE MIGHTY LION
SITTIN' THERE AND CRYIN'
BITTEN BY A TINY FLEA
MAMMOTH WAS COLOSSAL
WHAT'S HE NOW—A FOSSIL
BET YOUR LIFE I'M GLAD I'M ME!

WHAT'S STRONG IN BULK MAY LAG ALONG IN BRAINS AND HEART
THAT HANDSOME HULK MIGHT BE A
LILLIPUTIAN MENT'LY
PROVIN' CONSEQUENTLY . . .

THOUGH HE SHOWS YOU SHOULDERS
TWICE AS BIG AS BOULDERS
IF THE BRAIN'S A TINY PEA
WHEN YOU'RE IN A PICKLE
HE AIN'T WORTH A NICKEL
BET YOUR LIFE I'M GLAD I'M
BET YOUR LIFE I'M GLAD I'M
ME!

(*Beefeaters start off Left as Tom Thumb dances ending as once again we hear Ringmaster's voice*)

RINGMASTER'S VOICE: (*Over music*) . . . Ladies and gentlemen, together for the first time, Mr. P. T. Barnum's two Star Attractions—General Tom Thumb and—direct from the Royal Zoological Society of London—the King of All Pachyderms—Jumbo!

(*And Jumbo enters, so huge that all we see are four enormous legs as Beefeaters prod him into dance with Tom Thumb. Dance continues as Tom Thumb sings*)

TOM THUMB:

GIANTS LOOK SO AWESOME
FOLKS ARE SCARED TO CROSS 'EM
NONETHELESS I GUARANTEE
SMALLEST YANKEE DOODLE
IF HE'S IN THE MOOD'LL
BEAT THE WHOLE CABOODLE
USING JUST HIS NOODLE
BET YOUR LIFE I'M GLAD . . .

(Jumbo's ears and trunk have come in through this, Tom Thumb has climbed onto trunk, now exits as he sings)

I'M ME!

(End number as Tom Thumb rides off on Jumbo's trunk. Applause through end of which we hear sounds of trains approaching and departing as three drag clown passengers come on with baby and bottle, etc., as Ringmaster comes out Left)

RINGMASTER: . . . Once again in the Center Ring, Mr. P. T. Barnum versus the Female of the Species with Unheard-of, Unexpected, Alarming Results!

CHAIRY: *(Entering briskly Left, followed by Barnum, as we come up on Railroad Station, Boston, Massachusetts)* . . . Stuff and nonsense, Taylor! Tom Thumb may be the smallest man on earth but you managed to tell some pretty tall tales about him. *(Before Barnum can speak)* He's not a general and his name's no more Thumb than mine is.

BARNUM: I call that trimmin's, Chairy!

CHAIRY: Was Joice Heth's age trimmings too?

BARNUM: It was justice. I took all the years most women knock off their age and added it on to hers.

CHAIRY: Be that as it may, Mr. Barnum, if we have to be in the exhibition business at *least* you could find yourself one respectable attraction!

WELL-DRESSED GENTLEMAN: (*Starting across from Right to Left as Barnum protests,* "Now just a minute, Chairy . . .") Mr. Barnum, all my congratulations. (*Handing Barnum his card*) . . . Julius Goldschmidt. We met last autumn in New York and I caught your show here in Boston last night. Absolutely splendid!

BARNUM: Thank you, Mr. Goldschmidt. Chairy, you remember my mentioning Mr. Julius Goldschmidt. He's the gentleman who presented Mr. Booth on his last tour.

CHAIRY: Of course. What brings you to Boston, Mr. Goldschmidt?

GOLDSCHMIDT: Boston's home to me, Mrs. Barnum. I stopped off for a little visit before sailing to England to sign up that Swedish girl who's made such a stir over there.

CHAIRY: Jenny Lind! I read all about her, two command performances for the Queen!

BARNUM: Lind–Lind, of course! The India Rubber Lady who can tie a knot in her right arm.

GOLDSCHMIDT: (*Laughing*) Jenny Lind's an opera singer, Mr. Barnum, and according to all the critics her voice is the most glorious sound ever heard. But you'll get a chance to see for yourself when I present her first concert next fall at Castle Garden. (*Looking at his watch*) . . . Better get started. That New York train's due in a quarter of an hour . . . (*Shaking hands*) Mr. Barnum, Mrs. Barnum, a great pleasure and I look forward to seeing you in the fall.

CHAIRY: (*As Goldschmidt goes and Barnum looks after him, shaking his head*) What's the matter, Taylor?

BARNUM: Goldschmidt's a nice fellow and I don't like to see him lose his shirt.

CHAIRY: You don't think he'll be able to sign up Miss Lind?

BARNUM: That's just it, I'm afraid he will! And the American public's not gonna fill any hall just to hear a singer!

CHAIRY: I'm not so sure you're right, Taylor. You heard what he said . . . *two* command performances! It's high time *you* found yourself an attraction like that.

BARNUM: Now don't get started on *that* again or we'll miss the Chicago train. And besides, I wouldn't know how to begin!

CHAIRY: It's very simple. We toss a coin. Tails we continue as we are–Heads *I* run the rest of the tour and you go to England and make a deal with Miss Lind's agents.

BARNUM: (*Shocked*) Chairy! What would I say to Mr. Goldschmidt?

CHAIRY: That you were afraid New York would never buy an opera singer and you didn't want to see him lose his shirt.

BARNUM: I call that a lie, Chairy!

CHAIRY: I call that trimmings, Taylor. (*She tosses coin, looks at it*) . . . Bon voyage, Mr. Barnum.

BARNUM: Mrs. Barnum, this is uncharted territory!

CHAIRY: (*Starting off Left*) I'm equal to it, Taylor. And so are you.

BARNUM: Chairy, wait! (*Then to us*) . . . It wasn't too late, I still could've changed my mind, missed the New York train, followed Chairy west! But I didn't. I made the train, I made the boat, I made the deal. Now I had only one thing to figure out—who the hell was Jenny Lind? But like that fella Shakespeare said, what's in a name anyhow? It's titles the public wants! I'll call her the Scintillating Songbird from Scandinavia! (*Rejecting it*) The Scintillating Swedish Songbird. (*Another*) . . . The Songbird Who Scintillates from Sweden! (*Eureka*) I got it! (*Proudly*) . . . The Singing Swede. (*As he starts Off*) Unfortunately, Chairy'd already printed up the handbills so we were stuck with calling her the Swedish Nightingale. (*Exiting Left*) . . . You can't win 'em all.

(*Circus chase music up as Barnum exits and Ringmaster comes on Right*)

RINGMASTER: Ladies and gentlemen, for the First Time on these Blessed Shores, the world-renowned Living Statues! . . . Due to the extremely respectable nature of this attraction, Mr. Barnum's promotional campaign will avoid any sensational claims and rely upon the Plain Unvarnished Truth!

(*Ringmaster pulls down first banner reading "JENNY LIND DOES* NOT *WALK A WIRE TWO HUNDRED*

FEET ABOVE THE GROUND—WITHOUT A NET!", a second next to it reading "JENNY LIND WILL NOT *STEP INTO A CAGE OF FEROCIOUS BENGAL TIGERS", next to that a third reading "JENNY LIND DOES* NOT *GET SHOT OUT OF A CANNON", next to that a fourth reading "JENNY LIND DOES* NOT *EAT FIRE", next to that a fifth reading "JENNY LIND DOES* NOT *RIDE AN ELEPHANT", and next to that a sixth banner reading "JENNY LIND DOES* NOT *JUGGLE TWELVE FLAMING PINS AT ONCE". By this time banners have formed a solid curtain, and on last note of music, they fly out revealing the Living Statues supporting a frozen figure—facing Upstage—on their shoulders. Figure turns and we see it is a very beautiful young woman as Living Statues lower her to floor, exit Left and Right as Barnum starts on)*

BARNUM: (*Presenting her with bouquet of roses*) . . . P. T. Barnum, Miss Lind, welcoming you on behalf of one million two hundred thirty thousand citizens to the proud city of New York. (*She takes his hand*) Tell me, how was your crossing?

JENNY LIND: Vad säger ni?

BARNUM: Come again?

JENNY LIND: Förlåt, men jag förstår inte ert språk.

BARNUM: (*Beginning to be alarmed*) Miss Lind, this here is the United States of America! We speak English.

JENNY LIND: Engelska?

BARNUM: (*To assistant*) Henry, get me a hall! (*And we are on the bare stage of Castle Garden as he continues*) . . . Miss Lind, you've got to give a concert on this stage . . .

JENNY LIND: Ge en konsert.

BARNUM: (*A shout*) In English!

JENNY LIND: I no want learn English.

BARNUM: (*Leading her Left as set begins to change and we find ourselves on the bare stage of Castle Garden. Through course of the following he carefully enunciates each word and she repeats after him in a pronounced Swedish accent that grows lighter and lighter as words increase in speed like a locomotive chant*) You've got no choice!

JENNY LIND: Choosh?

BARNUM: Choice.

JENNY LIND: Choice.

BARNUM: That's good.

JENNY LIND: Gud.

BARNUM: Good.

JENNY LIND: Gud.

BARNUM: (*Lightly touching her arm*) Good.

JENNY LIND: (*Removing his hand*) No good!

BARNUM: That's it! Good evening . . .

JENNY LIND: Evening.

BARNUM: Evening.

JENNY LIND: Evening.

BARNUM: Evening.

JENNY LIND: Evening.

BARNUM: Evening, ladies . . .

JENNY LIND: Laddies.

BARNUM: Ladies.

JENNY LIND: Ladies.

BARNUM: Ladies.

JENNY LIND: Ladies.

BARNUM: Ladies and . . .

JENNY LIND: Und.

BARNUM: And.

JENNY LIND: Und.

BARNUM: And.

JENNY LIND: And.

BARNUM: And gentlemen.

JENNY LIND: (*Smiling*) Yentlemen.

BARNUM: Gentlemen.

JENNY LIND: Yentlemen.

BARNUM: Yentlemen.

JENNY LIND: Yentlemen.

BARNUM: No, *gentlemen!* (*Over sounds of orchestra tuning up*) . . . That'll have to do, I guess. And words they can't understand, we'll charge off to European style. And don't forget to smile! If there's one thing no American can resist, it's the smile of a beautiful woman . . . No American man anyhow. It's time to start so I'll be getting out into the house. (*As he starts off Right*) . . . Good luck!

JENNY LIND: Vad säger ni?

BARNUM: In English!

(*And as Barnum joins Chairy in Stage Right Box we hear last obbligato of Jenny Lind's concert and thunderous applause. The applause abates as Jenny looks at Barnum and very proudly says,* "Good evening, ladies and—yentlemen!" *More applause as Concertmaster joins her Onstage*)

CONCERTMASTER: (*After Jenny Lind has whispered to him*) . . . Ladies and gentlemen, Miss Lind thanks you for your kind reception of her program and asks if she might sing one last song. A song she performed at her first concert in Sweden and which she dedicates tonight to a new American friend. "Kärlek Oss till Dårskaper Leder."

(*A small string orchestra made up of clowns has assembled in half-light Down Left through above, and now softly plays the accompaniment as Jenny Lind sings*)

JENNY LIND:

BORT OM ALL GRÄNS
UTOM ALL TID
KÄRLEKENS LER OCH LOCKAR

KÄRLEKENS VIND
BRÄNNER SOM ELD
SPRÄNGER DEN HÖGSTA MUR

BORT OM ALL GRÄNS
UTOM ALL TID
KÄRLEKENS DÅRSKAP OSS FÖR

(Jenny Lind finishes the chorus in Swedish, then tentatively, hesitantly, she begins to sing in English)

LOVE KNOWS NO RULES
LOVE HAS NO TIME
LOVE LAUGHS AT RHYME AND REASON

SWEEPING THE STAGE
MAD OR SUBLIME
KNOWING NO AGE OR SEASON

WISE MEN AND FOOLS
PLAYING LOVE'S GAME
BEND TO THE SAME SWEET TREASON

LOVE'S SILVER SONG
SWIFT AS A FLAME
BREACHES THE STRONGEST WALL . . .

LOVE KNOWS NO RULES
LOVE HAS NO TIME
LOVE MAKES SUCH FOOLS
OF US ALL.

(End song, applause as crowd of well-wishers surround her. Barnum, in evening cape, stands to one side beaming. Suddenly she crosses to him)

JENNY LIND: . . . Mr. Barnum, I am a confusion. Many gentlemen ask go with me to the celebration tonight, and I not know which one to choose.

BARNUM: You pick whoever strikes your fancy, dear lady.

JENNY LIND: Very well, I choose a scholastic person. (*Reaching out for his hand, as Chairy starts on Right*) . . . My English Teacher.

BARNUM: (*Suddenly confused as Jenny Lind takes his hand*) Now my dear lady, *I* am a confusion . . .

CHAIRY: . . . Taylor, the carriage is waiting.

BARNUM: I'll be right along, Chairy . . .

JENNY LIND: (*Gently withdrawing her hand*) The mayor of the city, also he ask to escort me.

BARNUM: Look, Miss Lind . . .

CHAIRY: Taylor, please hurry, I want to freshen up at the hotel before the reception.

JENNY LIND: (*As music of* "Love Makes Such Fools of Us All" *comes softly up*) Oh well, perhaps another time.

BARNUM: (*As Jenny Lind starts Right, suddenly*) Chairy! (*Jenny Lind stops*) . . . Chairy, I got me a problem. The receipts, they've got to be counted again! Darn bookkeeper messed it all up, so you take that carriage and I'll catch up with you as soon as I can.

CHAIRY: (*Who understands*) This "bookkeeping" couldn't be done tomorrow, Taylor?

BARNUM: (*Not able to look at her*) No, Chairy. It can't.

CHAIRY: Very well, then. I'll see you . . . when I see you. (*Kissing him*) . . . It was a great success, Taylor. And I'm very proud of you. Good night, my darling. (*With a smile, as she exits*) Good night, Miss Lind.

BARNUM: (*As both ladies exit*) Chairy, wait! Miss Lind, I . . . (*Suddenly, to us*) . . . Well, dammit, why shouldn't I take her to the reception! Hell, it's just for a few hours! All my life I've been selling the dream to everybody else in the world, isn't it time I got a look at it myself? (*As pulse of music increases in intensity*) I'm a man! I got the price of admission! I wanna see what's going on inside the tent!! (*And he sings*)

STAYING HOME, LIVING DAY BY DAY
MAY BE SAFE BUT IT CAN'T BE DULLER
SEEING THINGS ONLY BLACK AND GRAY
WHEN THE WORLD IS ALIVE WITH COLOR
DOING JUST AS YOUR NEIGHBORS DO
MAY BE WISE BUT IT AIN'T SO CLEVER
EV'RY MAN HAS A DREAM OR TWO
LET 'EM GO AND THEY'RE GONE FOREVER

OUT THERE, SOMEWHERE, JUST OUT OF SIGHT
THERE'S A WORLD THAT'S BLAZING WITH LIGHT
AIN'T EACH MAN ALIVE GOT THE RIGHT
TO STRAY JUST A MITE FROM THE STRAIGHT AND NARROW
SHOOT THROUGH THE NIGHT LIKE A FLAMING ARROW

(*Through following, members of company begin rigging a tightrope wire from Stage Right Box to Stage Left Box and Jenny Lind appears in Box Right*)

TURNING BACK SHOULD THE HIGHWAY BEND
TURNING DOWN EV'RY CHANCE YOU'RE GIVEN

TAKES THE RISK OUT OF LIFE BUT FRIEND
HOW THE HELL CAN YOU CALL THAT LIVIN'?
STAYING PUT IN A PUMPKIN SHELL
IS A BLEAK AND DEPRESSING HABIT
THERE'S A RING ON THE CAROUSEL
AND IT'S YOURS IF YOU'LL ONLY GRAB IT

(*As he climbs into Stage Left Box*)

OUT THERE, SOMEWHERE, JUST DOWN THE LINE
LIES A WORLD OF GLORY AND SHINE
ONE SQUARE FOOT THERE'S GOTTA BE MINE . . .
ONCE IN HIS LIFE EV'RY MAN DECIDES
ONCE WHEN HE STANDS WHERE THE ROAD DIVIDES
ONCE ON A HILL AS THE MORNING GROWS
ONCE IF HE WILL HE CAN SEE THOSE

(*And he begins walking the wire*)

FIRES GLOW
FLAGS STREAMING
SPIRES GROW
TOW'RS GLEAMING
IN A LAND WHERE THE DAWN IS CLEAR
IN A SKY WHERE THE SUN'S FOREVER
ON A PLAIN WHERE IT'S SPRING ALL YEAR
AND THE DARK OF THE NIGHT COMES NEVER

(*He's almost there, Jenny Lind beckons him on*)

SOMEWHERE, OUT THERE, JUST OUT OF SIGHT
IN THAT WORLD THAT'S SHINING WITH LIGHT
AIN'T EACH MAN ALIVE GOT THE RIGHT

(*He does a low bow on wire, then steps into Stage Right Box*)

ONCE IN HIS LIFE TO FORGET THE PAST . . .

RINGMASTER: (*Coming on Right as music continues and double-hung trapeze flies in*) . . . In the Main Ring, ladies and gentlemen, the Latest International Sensation! The Rarest Most Beautiful Bird in Captivity—the Swedish Nightingale!

BARNUM: (*As Jenny Lind is helped down from Box and escorted to trapeze*)

ONCE IN HIS LIFE TO BEHOLD AT LAST . . .

RINGMASTER: (*Over music as Barnum climbs out of Box and joins Jenny Lind on trapeze*) . . . And Mr. Phineas Taylor Barnum in their Amazing Ascension Act with Gorgeous Pyrotechnic Display!

BARNUM: (*As trapeze lifts off*)

WITH HIS OWN TWO EYES
WHAT LIES
OUT THERE!

Music continues as we see the pyrotechnic display setting everything ablaze with sparkle and glitter as house lights come up on . . .

END OF ACT ONE

Act II

(As house lights start down Ringmaster comes Downstage, blows his whistle, and announces . . .)

RINGMASTER: . . . Out of the Main Ring, onto the Fairgrounds, for a Musical Salute celebrating Miss Jenny Lind's Fiftieth Concert in America, featuring the proud Citizens of Washington and the Potomac Marching Band.

COMPANY: *(Variously as they come down the aisles carrying banners, placards and signs reading "THE POTOMAC MARCHING BAND WELCOMES JENNY LIND", "THE NATION'S CAPITAL WELCOMES JENNY LIND", "WELCOME SWEDISH NIGHTINGALE", American flags, torches, sparklers, etc.)*

COME FOLLOW THE BAND
WHEREVER IT'S AT
LET BOTH OF YOUR FEET BEAT TIME TO THE DRUM
AND FEEL YOUR HEART GO RAT-A-TAT-TAT

A FLAG IN YOUR HAND
A PLUME IN YOUR HAT
BATTALIONS OF BRASS PASS AND CATCH THE LIGHT
IS THERE A SIGHT THAT'S SWEETER THAN THAT?

SEE THE PRETTY LADY TOSS THAT BATON HIGH
AIN'T SHE CUTE AS A DAISY?
WATCH THE FELLA WITH THE BIG BASS DRUM GO BY
AIN'T YOU GLAD THAT YOU STAYED?
HEAR THE TUBA PLAY THAT OOM-PAH-PAH, OH MY
AIN'T IT DRIVIN' YOU CRAZY?
DON'T YOU BE SO DARN LAZY
BETTER HURRY AND JOIN THAT BIG PARADE

UP OUTA YOUR SEAT
DOWN OFFA THE STAND
STEP OUT TO THE SWEET BEAT THE BUGLE PLAYS
A SOUND THAT YOU'LL REMEMBER ALL YOUR DAYS
AND WHEN YOU SEE THE LEADER PROUDLY RAISE
HIS HAND
JUST FOLLOW THE BAND!

MEMBERS OF THE BAND: (*Variously*)

HEAR THE TRUMPET BLAST
HEAR THE CORNET BLARE
HEAR THE BOOM OF THE BASS
AND THE RATTLE OF THE SNARE
WITH THE SWEETEST BURST OF MELODY I KNOW
(*INSTRUMENTAL*)—GOES THE PICCOLO!

HEAR THE SILVER TONE
OF THE XYLOPHONE
HEAR THE GLIDE AND THE BELLOW
OF THE SLIDE TROMBONE
THEN A BURST OF CRYSTAL, LISTEN TO IT PEAL
(*INSTRUMENTAL*)—IT'S THE GLOCKENSPIEL!

WITH A MOST MAJESTIC MANNER YOU'LL REMEMBER ALL YOUR LIFE
COMES MELLOPHONE
COMES SAXOPHONE

COMES SOUSAPHONE
COMES FIFE!

THEN THE BRASS SINGS OUT
THE WOODWINDS SIGH
THE TRUMPETS SHOUT
AND THE DRUMS REPLY
WITH A CRASH AND A CLANG AS THE WHOLE SHEBANG GOES BY!

(Orchestra section with piano. Chorus of song as Barnum appears in Stage Left Box dressed in clown costume as he throws handbills into audience announcing "FREE JENNY LIND CONCERT ON WHITE HOUSE LAWN TONIGHT", and sings)

BARNUM:

SEE THE PRETTY LADY TOSS THAT BATON HIGH
AIN'T SHE CUTE AS A DAISY?
WATCH THE FELLA WITH THE BIG BASS DRUM GO BY
AIN'T YOU GLAD THAT YOU STAYED?
HEAR THE TUBA PLAY THAT OOM-PAH-PAH, OH MY
AIN'T IT DRIVIN' YOU CRAZY?
DON'T YOU BE SO DARN LAZY
BETTER HURRY AND JOIN THAT BIG PARADE

(As full company join him)

COME FOLLOW THE BAND
. . . COME FOLLOW THE BAND
WHEREVER IT'S AT
. . . WHEREVER IT'S AT
LET BOTH OF YOUR FEET BEAT TIME TO THE DRUM
AND FEEL YOUR HEART GO RAT-A-TAT-TAT
A FLAG IN YOUR HAND

. . . A FLAG IN YOUR HAND
A PLUME IN YOUR HAT
. . . A PLUME IN YOUR HAT

(*As Barnum and lady clown come Down Center, continue passing out handbills*)

BATTALIONS OF BRASS PASS AND CATCH THE LIGHT
IS THERE A SIGHT THAT'S SWEETER THAN THAT?

BARNUM: (*Over music*) . . . Ladies and gentlemen, good citizens of Washington, and esteemed members of the Potomac Marching Band Society. President and Mrs. Fillmore respectfully invite each of you to join them on the White House lawn this evening where Miss Jenny Lind will make her first appearance in our nation's Capital!

COMPANY: (*Softly continuing under above*)

SEE THE PRETTY LADY TOSS THAT BATON HIGH
AIN'T SHE CUTE AS A DAISY?
WATCH THE FELLA WITH THE BIG BASS DRUM GO BY
AIN'T YOU GLAD THAT YOU STAYED?
HEAR THE TUBA PLAY THAT OOM-PAH-PAH, OH MY
AIN'T IT DRIVIN' YOU CRAZY?

(*As Barnum throws last handbills into audience*)

DON'T YOU BE SO DARN LAZY
BETTER HURRY AND JOIN THAT BIG PARADE

BARNUM/COMPANY:

UP OUTA YOUR SEAT
. . . UP OUTA YOUR SEAT!
DOWN OFFA THE STAND
. . . DOWN OFFA THE STAND!
STEP OUT TO THE SWEET BEAT THE BUGLE PLAYS

A SOUND THAT YOU'LL REMEMBER ALL YOUR DAYS
AND WHEN YOU HEAR THE LEADER PROUDLY RAISE
HIS HAND . . .
JUST FOLLOW THE BAND!

(End song, applause, Barnum continues singing to accompaniment of one-man band as company exit and Wilton comes on)

BARNUM:

COME FOLLOW THE BAND
WHEREVER IT'S AT
LET BOTH OF YOUR FEET BEAT TIME TO THE DRUM . . .

WILTON: Sir . . .

BARNUM: *(Pointedly ignoring him)*

AND FEEL YOUR HEART GO RAT-A-TAT-TAT
A FLAG IN YOUR HAND . . .

WILTON: Sir, it's nearly six-fifteen . . .

BARNUM: *(Louder)*

A PLUME IN YOUR HAT
BATTALIONS OF BRASS PASS AND CATCH THE LIGHT
IS THERE A SIGHT THAT'S SWEETER THAN THAT?

(One-man band slaps Barnum with slapstick and as Barnum falls flat on his face, one-man band exits Left)

BARNUM: Dammit, Wilton, don't I even get *one* evening off?

WILTON: Miss Lind asked me to remind you that the reception's at seven o'clock sharp and since President Fillmore is a stickler for punctuality . . .

BARNUM: (*As Wilton helps him undress*) Whole six months of this tour's been nothing but tea with the President, reception for the Chief Justice, supper with the Senator, when do they find time to run the country? (*Suddenly*) . . . So help me, Wilton, I'd give up the whole tour just to get away from them!

WILTON: You don't mean that, Mr. Barnum.

BARNUM: (*As he continues taking off costume*) I do! Old Goldschmidt's been after me to buy her contract and I've a good mind to sell it to him. Oh it was fine in the beginning when we had to turn an opera singer into a Swedish Nightingale, but now the only thing I'm getting out of that bird is money and it's not enough! (*Getting up*) . . . My own damn fault! I humbugged myself into thinking I needed some more color in my life, and she humbugged me into being respectable—a miserable state of affairs as far as I'm concerned—so I might as well be miserable being respectable with someone I love.

WILTON: But I thought you and Miss Lind . . .

BARNUM: So did I. But I was wrong. (*Getting up*) . . . Look, you'd better send a wire to Goldschmidt telling him I'll meet him in New York day after tomorrow. And another to Mrs. Barnum telling her if that coin comes up heads—I might just be in Bridgeport end of next week! (*To us, as Wilton exits, and Jenny Lind puts finishing touches to her makeup at dressing table that comes on from Left*) This is gonna be a waste of time, I know that. None of my "female of the species" humbugs seem to pan out, but I'm too old a dog not to try. (*As he angrily washes face, begins mumbling to himself*) . . . Never heard of such carryings on! And in public! It's a disgrace if you ask me . . .

JENNY LIND: (*Having a good idea of what he's up to*) Phineas, are you muttering?

BARNUM: Me? Absolutely not! I think muttering's the height of impoliteness . . .

JENNY LIND: Then I'll just ignore it.

BARNUM: (*Muttering away*) I never mutter, I might sputter but I don't mutter, when I got something to say that matters, I don't mutter, I utter—But it's still a damn disgrace!

JENNY LIND: I bet I know what this is about. The way the French Ambassador smiled at me last night.

BARNUM: Wrong! What do I care if some weaselly-lookin' Frenchie smiles at you! (*Giving up*) . . . It's the way you smiled at him. One of your Number Two special trembly ones.

JENNY LIND: (*Laughing*) Phineas, I'm a soprano and we flirt. The way impresarios mutter. Anyway, what's sauce for the goose is sauce for the gander.

BARNUM: What are you talking about?

JENNY LIND: The letters.

BARNUM: What letters?

JENNY LIND: Long ones. Daily. To a lady in Bridgeport, Connecticut. Now if you were willing to give up these letters, I might be willing to give up my "trembly" smiles.

BARNUM: (*After a moment, as music comes softly up*) Jenny, I want you to know I'll never forget you.

JENNY LIND: (*Realizing what he means*) It has been a lovely six months. (*Starting to wardrobe rack*) . . . Jag önskar dig allt det du drömmer om, Phineas. In English—I want for you what you want for yourself.

BARNUM: That's a kind wish, Jenny. Now I've got to figure out what the devil it is I want!

JENNY LIND: (*With just a touch of regret*) Well at least we know what it isn't. (*And as Barnum takes out valise and begins packing, she softly sings*)

THIS GAME OF LOVE
AMUSES
UNLESS OF COURSE
ONE LOSES . . .

(*As music continues*) . . . When do you think you'll be leaving?

BARNUM: I suppose tonight's as good a time as any. Will you be all right?

JENNY LIND: I think so. I have a dinner engagement . . . with the French Ambassador. (*As she starts Left*)

WISE MEN AND FOOLS
PLAYING LOVE'S GAME
BEND TO THE SAME SWEET TREASON . . .

BARNUM: (*As music continues, Goldschmidt comes on Right, and Jenny Lind dresses Left*) . . . Look at those figures for St. Louis, sold out two months before she ever sets foot in town. You're buying a songbird that lays golden eggs, Mr. Goldschmidt.

GOLDSCHMIDT: I know that, Mr. Barnum. In fact, you might say I knew it before you did.

BARNUM: That's why I'm making you such a generous deal. Only one proviso—if Miss Lind ever plays Bridgeport, don't sell me any seats. (*Putting out his hand*) . . . Done?

GOLDSCHMIDT: Done.

(*Through course of this Jenny Lind has removed her dressing gown revealing circus tights as Goldschmidt goes off and two strongmen lift Jenny Lind as she sings*)

JENNY LIND:

LOVE MAKES SUCH FOOLS
OF US ALL . . .

(*Barnum watches as Jenny Lind vanishes and Chairy appears in her place*)

BARNUM: . . . Why, Chairy Barnum, what are you doing here?

CHAIRY: (*Holding out coin*) It came up heads. And I still think you're beautiful. (*Gently*) . . . My way this time, Taylor.

BARNUM: (*As he takes out red napkin from Women's Emporium scene, turns it gray, and hands it to Chairy*) Your way.

(*And they embrace as Ringmaster appears in House Left Box with rifle*)

RINGMASTER: (*As he shoots out colored lights*) . . . Out of the Tent, away from the Midway, without the benefit of Kelly Green, Buttercup Yellow, or Cherry Red; the Bridgeport Grand Opera and Pageant Company presents Mr. P. T. Barnum as he lives his life in . . .

BLUES SINGER: (*As proscenium arch and grand drape of Hawe's Opera House, Bridgeport, comes in. Drape represents front page of Bridgeport* Courrier, *May 7, 1851. Headline splashed across the top reads "BARNUM SURRENDERS!" with period caricatures of Tom Thumb, Jenny Lind, Joice Heth, Mermaid, etc. weeping at Barnum's departure from the exhibition business*)

BLACK AND WHITE
THE FUTURE'S ROSY
LIVIN' BLACK AND WHITE
KEEP BOTH FEET ON THE GROUND
DON'T LET THOSE DAYDREAMS SPIN YOU ROUND
SEE THINGS THE WAY THEY ARE
YOU'RE GONNA TUMBLE IF YOU FLY TOO FAR
STAY LOW AND HOLD ON TIGHT
LIVIN' BLACK AND WHITE

CHAIRY/CHOIR: (*As curtain rises on choir posed as clockworks*)

MAY THE SEVENTH, EIGHTEEN FIFTY-ONE
DAY OF DAYS FOR BRIDGEPORT'S FAV'RITE SON
LIVING WHALES HE'S SENT TO HADES
LIKEWISE SWEDISH SINGING LADIES
AND THE LOCAL CLOCKWORKS HE WILL RUN . . .

(*Clockworks set in motion on* last of this *and Barnum turns a screw, winds a key, pulls a lever, shoves a cuckoo back in a hole—then starts all over again. Faster and faster goes the tempo until he is caught up in his own machinery as Curtain comes down and Chairy and choir come back on*)

CHAIRY/CHOIR:

HE COULD RUN A CLOCKWORKS, BARNUM FOUND
IN TWO MONTHS HE'D RUN IT IN THE GROUND
PURCHASED THEN FIVE HUNDRED SHOVELS

SAID "MEN MUSTN'T LIVE IN HOVELS
AND A NEW UTOPIA I WILL FOUND!"

(Choir exit behind curtain as Chairy continues)

CHAIRY:

PLANNED A VERY MODERN MODEL TOWN
ELEVATED ROADS TO STROLL AROUN'
ROOFS SO HIGH IT MAKES YOU GROGGY
BUILT ON LAND A TRIFLE SOGGY
SO AS IT ROSE UP, IT STARTED DOWN . . .

BLUES SINGER: *(As curtain rises on choir posed as buildings in Barnum City. Through following, "buildings" begin sinking)*

BLACK AND WHITE
HE BUILT A CITY THAT WAS
BLACK AND WHITE
IT TOOK NO END OF SPUNK
AND LOOKED QUITE SPLENDID AS IT SUNK
HERE COMES ANOTHER LURCH
THERE GOES THE DEPOT AND THE BAPTIST CHURCH
AS THEY SLIPPED OUT OF SIGHT
THEY WERE BLACK AND WHITE
SO LONG, TA-TA, GOOD NIGHT
BYE-BYE BLACK AND WHITE
WHITE . . .
OH YEAH

(Barnum has tried propping sinking "buildings" through above, now as last one disappears, Chairy and choir return)

CHAIRY/CHOIR:

HEARD ABOUT YOUR CITY, WHAT A SHAME!
BUT THE TRUTH IS POLITICS YOUR GAME
KISSING BABIES, MAKING SPEECHES

POSING WITH THE LOCAL PEACHES
FUN, RESPECTABILITY, AND FAME

YOU COULD BE AN ALDERMAN, NO WAIT
CONGRESSMAN, I MEAN U.S., NOT STATE!
MAYOR, NO, THAT'S EASY PICKIN'S
SENATOR, OH WHAT THE DICKENS
WHY NOT HEAD OUR PRESIDENTIAL SLATE?

BLUES SINGER: *(As Barnum and Chairy step onto platform up center and members of choir gather round them)*

BLACK AND WHITE
HE'S PLAYING POLITICS IN
BLACK AND WHITE
COLD TRUTH AND GOOD HARD FACTS
GIVE ALL THAT RAZZ-MA-TAZZ THE AXE
NO BUNTING IN THE STREETS
HE'LL TALK OF BUDGET CUTS
AND BALANCE SHEETS
STATISTICS DAY AND NIGHT
RUNNING BLACK AND WHITE

BARNUM: *(As through this crowd applauds, shouts, jeers, cheers)*

HERE'S MY STAND ON WOMEN'S RIGHTS
I'M FOR 'EM!
SLAVERY IN ANY FORM'S
A NAY
TAXES HAVE TO BE INCREASED
TO HELP THE FOLKS WHO HAVE THE LEAST
TOBACCO I WOULD BAN
AS OF TODAY
I'M PROUD TO SAY HOORAY
FOR UNIVERSAL SUFFRAGE
AND THAT MEANS BLACK AND WHITE

AS WELL AS HE AND SHE
WITH VOTES FOR BLACKS AND WOMEN FOLKS
A RISE IN TAX, A BAN ON SMOKES
HOW COULD YOU VOTE FOR ANYONE BUT ME?

(*As through this people start to walk away until only Chairy is left listening to him*)

BLACK AND WHITE
I'M PLAYING POLITICS IN
BLACK AND WHITE
COLD TRUTH AND GOOD HARD FACTS
GIVE ALL THAT RAZZ-MA-TAZZ THE AXE . . .

(*As music continues*) . . . Chairy, I'm losing 'em! They're gettin away! You've got to let me bring some color into this campaign or they're gonna beat me! Chairy, you gotta release me from my promise!

CHAIRY: (*A moment, then she takes gray napkin from Emporium scene, turns it red, and hands it to Barnum*) Go ahead, Taylor.

(*Barnum blows whistle, and at that moment Hawes Opera House flies out and clowns come racing on with balloons, confetti, and bolts of colored fabric—red, green, yellow, blue, gold—which transformed the entire set into a riot of color as balloons are sent sailing out into the audience and full company sings*)

FULL COMPANY: (*As through this two clowns appear Right and unroll huge banner reading: "CONGRATULATIONS MAYOR P. T. BARNUM"*)

BLACK AND WHITE
HE'S HAD HIS FILL OF
LIVIN' BLACK AND WHITE
SO LONG, TA-TA, GOOD NIGHT

BYE-BYE BYE-BYE
BLACK AND
WHITE!

(*End number, applause as company exit Right and Left and Blues Singer appears in Stage Left Box*)

BLUES SINGER: (*As set begins to change*)

BLACK AND WHITE
HE'S HAD HIS FILL OF
LIVIN' BLACK AND WHITE
SO LONG, TA-TA, GOOD NIGHT
BYE-BYE BLACK AND
WHITE . . .

(*As music continues*) . . . Outside the Tent, After the Show, Behind the Scenes. Beneath the Makeup.

(*And she exits as lights come up on steps of the City Hall, Bridgeport, Connecticut. It is evening and Barnum and Chairy start on Right*)

CHAIRY: . . . Taylor, wait a minute.

BARNUM: What's the matter, dear?

CHAIRY: Nothing. I just need to rest for a moment.

BARNUM: You know what, Chairy, so do I. Let's sit down for a spell.

CHAIRY: On the steps of the City Hall? It's illegal!

BARNUM: Well, that'll be my first act as Mayor—to get a law passed that all elected officials with beautiful wives can rest on the steps of the City Hall as long as I'm in office. (*As he helps her sit down*) . . . How's that?

CHAIRY: Thank you very much, Mr. Barnum.

BARNUM: (*Sitting beside her*) You're entirely welcome, Mrs. Barnum. Impressive place, isn't it?

CHAIRY: The most respectable-looking building I've ever seen! And it belongs to you now.

BARNUM: You know, Chairy, lookin' at you smiling here in the dark makes me think of that first night we met in that thunderstorm. I know you were scared, but I kept wishin' there would be more lightnin' so I could get another look at your face.

CHAIRY: And I shut my eyes every time the lightnin' flashed, so I never did get a good look at yours till we were standing at the altar. And by then it was too late. (*They laugh. He takes her hand*) . . . Now, Taylor, stop it. Folks are gonna think we're foolish.

BARNUM: Why?

CHAIRY: Two old people sittin' on these steps in the middle of the night holding hands.

BARNUM: Who says we're old? Oh, maybe I got a few gray hairs and some laugh lines, but, Chairy, you don't look a day older than you did when I took you home in that thunderstorm.

CHAIRY: I thought you were through with humbug!

BARNUM: Twenty-two or three at the most. And that's the least humbugging thing I have ever said in my life!

CHAIRY: (*Hugging his arm*) You're going to be wonderful in politics, Taylor. Course I don't expect you to be Mayor more than one term. I've already got my eye on a Senate seat. And not the State Senate either . . .

BARNUM: Chairy, you're talkin' about Washington!

CHAIRY: (*Taking coin from her purse*) Heads say you can do it, Taylor.

BARNUM: Deciding to run for the U. S. Senate's nothin' you toss a coin on, it takes pondering and considering and contemplating . . . (*Suddenly*) . . . And how come in twenty-five years of tossing, that coin never once came up tails?

CHAIRY: I guess Fate is just on my side, Taylor. (*Then turning over coin*) . . . That and the fact that this quarter just happens to have two heads.

BARNUM: You stacked the deck, Chairy!

CHAIRY: I haven't been watchin' you twenty-five years for nothing, Taylor.

BARNUM: (*As music comes up*) All right, Mrs. Barnum, I'll run for your damn Senate because I love you and would do anything in the world to make you happy, but you have humbugged me good and proper and I am most displeased! Why are you smiling?

CHAIRY: (*Taking his hand*) Everything's going to be all right. We're quarreling again. (*And joined by Barnum, her lines in italics, she sings*)

The colors of my life
THE COLORS OF MY LIFE
Are softer than a breeze
ARE BOUNTIFUL AND BOLD

THE PURPLE GLOW OF INDIGO
The silver-gray of eiderdown
THE GLEAM OF GREEN AND GOLD
The dappled green of trees
THE SPLENDOR OF A SUNRISE
The amber of a wheatfield
THE DAZZLE OF A FLAME
The hazel of a seed
THE GLORY OF A RAINBOW
The crystal of a raindrop
I'D PUT 'EM ALL TO SHAME
Are all I'll ever need
NO QUIET BROWNS AND GRAYS
Your reds are much too bold
I'LL TAKE MY DAYS INSTEAD
In gold I find no worth
AND FILL THEM TILL THEY OVERFLOW
I'll fill my days with sage and brown
WITH ROSE AND CHERRY RED
The colors of the earth . . .

BARNUM: (*As eight jugglers appear behind them*)

AND IF FROM BY MY SIDE
MY LOVE SHOULD ROAM

CHAIRY: (*As she takes three balls from jugglers, holds them out so it seems she is about to hand them to Barnum, then suddenly begins to juggle them herself as other jugglers join her*)

THE COLORS OF MY LIFE
WILL SHINE A QUIET LIGHT
TO LEAD HIM HOME

(*Music continues as she tosses the balls to Barnum who begins juggling as Chairy and six jugglers exit*)

BARNUM: (*As he juggles*) . . . Chairy. (*She is gone*) Chairy! (*A shout as he throws balls away*) . . . Chairy!

(*He turns Upstage and two remaining jugglers stop juggling and exit, revealing Templeton and Morrissey in mourning dress*)

MORRISSEY: . . . On behalf of the Party, Mr. Barnum, may I say how sorry we are.

BARNUM: Month after month of standing right there beside me, then just when we're right on the threshold . . . (*Calming their fears*) . . . Now I don't want you boys to worry 'cause during this campaign I'm gonna be stronger than ever! I've worked a long time for the Senatorial nomination and it's an election I don't plan to lose.

TEMPLETON: Mr. Barnum, I'm afraid that there's been a slight postponement on your nomination.

BARNUM: What are you talking about?

MORRISSEY: What Mr. Templeton's trying to say is that the Party's position has changed. We're giving the nomination to Alexander Whittaker.

BARNUM: What are you talking about? I've been barnstorming for the past six months on the strength of your promise that I'd have that nomination.

TEMPLETON: The decision's out of our hands, Mr. Barnum! But in four years you'll be a prime candidate.

BARNUM: (*A shout*) I don't want the nomination in four years! I promised somebody I'd be in Washington next January and if I can't be there then, I don't want to be there at all. Good day.

TEMPLETON: But, Mr. Barnum . . .

BARNUM: Get out! (*They exit leaving Barnum alone on the stage*) . . . They took me, Chairy. Six months of making speeches and they take the nomination away from me with a lie worse than any humbug I ever pulled in thirty-five years of fooling people! I thought I'd got it out of my life, but I was wrong 'cause it looks like if I don't humbug them, they're gonna do worse to me. And, Chairy, tell the truth, is humbug so bad after all? Look at that shipload of reubens come over on the *Mayflower;* they were humbugged with a dream of findin' some kind of utopia and it turned out pretty good. And Tom Jefferson and Ben Franklin back in '76. Humbugged with a vision of makin' a whole society of free and equal people and that dream of theirs was strong enough to win a war! Course I'm not comparin' live mermaids and four-headed frogs to the Declaration of Independence, but somewhere way down deep there's a connection . . . (*Realizing what he's said as music comes up*) . . . How do you like that? I haven't lost my touch after all! Up here on a soap box for two minutes and I convinced myself I'm first cousins with Thomas Jefferson. Well, darn it, Chairy, don't that prove it? At humbuggin' I'm the best there is! (*And he sings*)

THE PRINCE OF HUMBUG!
BALDERDASH
FIDDLE-FADDLE
DRIVEL, TOSH
TWIDDLE-TWADDLE
BLATHER, BOSH
BILGE AND DODGE AND DOUBLE DUTCH
AND FLIM-FLAM
I AM!

THE KING OF HOGWASH
TOMMYROT

GIBBER, JABBER,
BLABBER, BLUFF
HOCUS-POCUS
GABBLE, GUFF
SCAM AND SHAM AND JUST A TOUCH
OF WHITE LIE
AM I!

DUKE OF TRIPE AND IDLE CHAT
EARL OF OIL
LORD OF BLAT
EMPEROR OF RIGMAROLE
THAT I AM!
BLESS MY SOUL!

THE PRINCE OF HUMBUG!
POPPYCOCK
PIFFLE, WAFFLE
PATTER, JUNK
HOKUM, HOOEY
CHATTER, BUNK
WILE AND GUILE
AND TRUMPERY . . .
THAT'S ME!

(*As music continues*) . . . Oh, don't worry, Chairy, I'm not going back into the menagerie business. What I was thinkin' about was a lecture tour. Tell the whole country about the Noble Art of Humbug. And who's got a better right to talk about it than me? After all, it's the thing God gave me the gift for, and it's how I got everything I ever had! Even you. (*And he sings*)

IN A WORLD OF STING AND SHOCK, THIS MOMENT WE SPEND
DOWN A ROAD OF RIDGE AND ROCK TOWARD LORD KNOWS WHAT END

THROUGH A NIGHT AS COLD AS SPACE AND DARK AS THE SEA
SOMEONE'S GOT TO MAKE IT BRIGHT
SHOOT A ROCKET, SHINE A LIGHT
TELL YOU WHO THAT SOMEONE'S GONNA BE . . .

THE PRINCE OF HUMBUG
TONGUE IN CHEEK
SHILLY-SHALLY
PULL THE WOOL
BLARNEY, BOGUS
COCK AND BULL
HOAX AND PRANK AND HANKY-PANK
AND SOME SKULLDUGGERY . . .

I AM!
AND DAMN I'LL ALWAYS BE!

RINGMASTER: . . . The Main Event! The Greatest Contest of Them All! P. T. Barnum, Unarmed, Alone, Without a Net . . . in a Struggle to the Finish—with Destiny! (*He takes off his Ringmaster hat and crosses to Barnum*) Bailey's the name, Mr. Barnum, and I'm here for my three-thirty appointment.

BARNUM: Sorry, Mr. Bailey, I've given the matter a great deal of thought and I'm afraid the answer's no.

BAILEY: Mr. Barnum, I sent those plans and photographs last week, didn't you get a chance to see them?

BARNUM: I saw the pictures, and your menagerie doesn't look too bad, but I've been out of the business for years and I'm not thinking of going back in it. But if you don't mind a bit of advice . . .

BAILEY: I'd welcome it . . .

BARNUM: You got to hook your attractions to the mood of the country! It's 1880 and with Grant in the White House we're expanding our boundaries! Your show looks good, but it's too small! There oughta be ten elephants, twenty clowns, plus acrobats, bareback riders, fat ladies, a whole family of jugglers, six up on the high wire!

BAILEY: Impossible! You couldn't get all those acts into one ring.

BARNUM: Put a couple of more rings on either side! And a band of forty pieces, with a whole separate tent for sideshows. Not to mention traveling grandstands you can put up and take down to seat five thousand people and a special train with two locomotives and sixty cars and enough canvas to put the entire Crystal Palace inside and still have room left over to fly a kite!

BAILEY: The Crystal Palace! Mr. Barnum, I hope I'm not bein' humbugged.

BARNUM: Mr. Bailey, whatever gave you that idea?

BAILEY: Well, I must admit it does sound good the way you tell it . . . but you've got to help me!

BARNUM: Out of the question.

BAILEY: I need you! The circus needs you!

BARNUM: No!

BAILEY: (*Singing*)

WHEN THE PILL THE DOCTOR GAVE YOU
TURNS YOUR COLD TO THE GRIPPE

WHEN A STITCH TO SAVE NINE OTHERS
COMES APART WITH A RIP
WHEN THE RATS INVADE YOUR ATTIC
AND START LEAVING YOUR SHIP
FOLLOW MY TIP
COME AWAY ON A TRIP . . .

JUST JOIN THE CIRCUS
LIKE YOU WANTED TO
WHEN YOU WERE A KID
CLIMB ABOARD
BEFORE IT MOVES ON AND YOU'LL
THANK YOUR LUCKY STARS YOU DID
GO TO BED IN MINNEAPOLIS
WAKE UP IN P.A.
PACK YOUR ROLL, YOUR BRUSH AND YOUR COMB AGAIN
READY TO ROAM AGAIN
READY TO STRAY
BLESS YOUR SOUL, YOU'LL NEVER GO HOME AGAIN
WHEN THE CIRCUS COMES YOUR WAY!

BARNUM: (*As music continues*) . . . It's no use! I just can't do it! Try the Sells Brothers!

(*And he starts off Right as three clowns bound on Right, blocking his path as they sing*)

THREE CLOWNS:

WHEN YOU'VE PATCHES IN YOUR TROUSERS
AND A HOLE IN YOUR PURSE
WHEN YOUR NINE TO FIVE IS BORING
AND YOUR FIVE TO NINE'S WORSE
WHEN YOU SNEEZE INSTEAD OF "BLESS YOU"
YOU GET JEERS AND A CURSE
DON'T CALL A HEARSE
WHILE YOU STILL GOT THE CHERCE . . .

(As through the following Barnum tries to exit in various directions, each time being stopped by more and more circus performers who push him back into the center of the ring as they sing)

JUST JOIN THE CIRCUS
LIKE YOU MEANT TO DO
WHEN YOU WERE SO HIGH
PITCH YOUR TROUBLES
UNDER A TENT AND YOU'RE
BOUND TO LOSE 'EM BY AND BY

SAY SO LONG TO FAIR SCHENECTADY
GREET SWEET SANTA FE
TOSS YOUR HAT AND CANE IN A SACK AGAIN
SHOULDER YOUR PACK AND THEN
HITCH UP THE SHAY
KISS THE CAT AND NEVER LOOK BACK AGAIN
WHEN THE CIRCUS COMES YOUR WAY!

BAILEY/FULL COMPANY: *(Variously, as Barnum mumbles,* "Now see here, Mr. Bailey, I appreciate your offer, but I've already told you I'm presently retired from the business and I'm not lookin' to jump into anything right now, etc.")

WHEN THE LADY YOU BEEN COURTIN'
WEDS YOUR BROTHER INSTEAD
WHEN HIS HONOR GIVES YOU THIRTY DAYS
ON WATER AND BREAD
WHEN YOUR BANK ACCOUNT'S A MILLION
BUT IT'S ALL IN THE RED
DON'T LOSE YOUR HEAD
PIN THIS NOTE TO THE BED . . .

I'VE JOINED THE CIRCUS
LIKE I WANTED TO

WHEN I WAS A KID
CLIMBED ABOARD
BEFORE IT MOVED ON AND YOU
BET YOUR LIFE I'M GLAD I DID
WENT TO BED IN MINNEAPOLIS
WOKE UP IN P.A.
PACKED MY ROLL, MY BRUSH, AND MY COMB AGAIN
READY TO ROAM AGAIN
SHOW ME THE WAY
BLESS MY SOUL, I'LL NEVER GO HOME AGAIN
WHEN THE CIRCUS COMES MY WAY . . .

(Bailey, then one by one, all performers, as they surround Barnum)

SEE THAT TENT POLE SLOWLY START TO RISE
CIRCUS!
CIRCUS!
JUST TO SAY THE WORD ELECTRIFIES
CIRCUS!
CIRCUS!
SEE THAT TIGER
SHAKIN' HANDS
LIKE A PUP THERE
THAT LADY
DANCING ON A WIRE
A MILLION MILES UP THERE

THAT STRING OF PAINTED CARS DOWN RAILROAD AVENUE
CIRCUS!
CIRCUS!
TWO PINK PASTEBOARDS SAY YOU'RE GOING TO
CIRCUS!
CIRCUS!
SHARE THE GLAD TIMES AND THE WOE WITH US
PACK YOUR TRUNK AND JOIN THE SHOW WITH US
ROLL FROM MAINE TO KOKOMO WITH US
MR. BARNUM SAY YOU'LL GO WITH US . . .

BARNUM: (*As company repeats,* "Join the circus!") . . . All right, dammit, why don't we leave it up to the Fates? (*Taking out Chairy's coin*) Heads it's yes, tails it's no. (*He tosses it*) . . . Mr. Bailey, you got yourself a partner.

BAILEY: To the biggest show in the country!

BARNUM: To the greatest show on earth!

BAILEY/FULL COMPANY: WHEN THE CIRCUS COMES YOUR WAY!

(*Number develops into the Greatest Show on Earth complete with jugglers, high-wire acts, trapeze artists, "wild animals," etc. as Barnum, now transformed into the ultimate Ringmaster with red-sequined jacket, white britches, and black riding boots, steps Down Center and sings*)

BARNUM:

I'VE JOINED THE CIRCUS
LIKE I WANTED TO
WHEN I WAS A KID
CLIMBED ABOARD
BEFORE IT MOVED ON AND YOU
BET YOUR LIFE I'M GLAD I DID
WENT TO BED IN MINNEAPOLIS
WOKE UP IN P.A.
PACKED MY ROLL, MY BRUSH, AND MY COMB AGAIN
READY TO ROAM AGAIN
SHOW ME THE WAY
BLESS MY SOUL I'LL NEVER GO HOME AGAIN
FROM THE DAY I JOIN THE

BARNUM/FULL COMPANY:

CIRCUS!
BE PROUD TO SAY YOU'LL JOIN THE

CIRCUS!
STEP RIGHT THIS WAY AND JOIN THE
CIRCUS!
JUST STICK A BANNER IN YOUR HAND
AND
JOIN THE CIRCUS LIKE YOU WANTED TO
LIKE YOU ALWAYS WANTED TO
RUN AWAY!

(*End number, applause as company start down the aisles and Barnum announces . . .*)

BARNUM: . . . Ladies and gentlemen, the Greatest Show on Earth is proud to present Madame Boissevan and her world-famous prancing Arabian ponies ++++ To your left Lady Francesca will swallow two flaming torches as she leaps through the circle of fire ++++ To your right, Signor Vivalla of Genoa, Italy, the amazing human cannonball ++++ And now the king of the jungle, Anton Vladimirovich and his royal African lions ++++ Ladies and gentlemen, the internationally celebrated sisters of the high wire, the amazing and daring Lilly and Lisa ++++ And in the Center Ring, the greatest spectacle of them all, the world-renowned Barnum and Bailey elephant parade!

FULL COMPANY: (*In aisles, through above*)

JOIN THE CIRCUS
LIKE YOU WANTED TO
WHEN YOU WERE A KID
CLIMB ABOARD
BEFORE IT MOVES ON AND YOU'LL
THANK YOUR LUCKY STARS YOU DID
GO TO BED IN MINNEAPOLIS
WAKE UP IN P.A.
PACK YOUR ROLL, YOUR BRUSH, AND YOUR COMB AGAIN
READY TO ROAM AGAIN

READY TO STRAY
BLESS YOUR SOUL, YOU'LL NEVER GO HOME AGAIN
FROM THE DAY YOU JOIN THE
CIRCUS!
BE PROUD TO SAY YOU'LL JOIN THE
CIRCUS!
STEP RIGHT THIS WAY AND JOIN THE
CIRCUS!
JUST STICK A BANNER IN YOUR HAND
AND
JOIN THE CIRCUS LIKE YOU WANTED TO
LIKE YOU ALWAYS WANTED TO
RUN AWAY!

(*End number, applause, and as lights begin to fade Barnum walks Upstage Center*)

CHAIRY: (*Appearing in Stage Right Box, the final Ringmaster*) . . . In the Center Ring, a Princely Final Attraction, Mr. Phineas Taylor Barnum himself!

BARNUM: (*As lights begin to fade and music of "Sucker" sneaks softly up*) 'Course that was a long time ago. And Joice Heth is gone and forgotten. And so's the American Museum and the living whale and Jenny Lind and my poor Tom Thumb. And them reubens that came over on the *Mayflower* have gone to dust, and Tom Jefferson's a memory, and old Franklin's flown his last kite. So my kind of humbug's disappeared . . . (*Shaking his head*) . . . Pity.

(*He tips his hat, lights go swiftly down as he exits singing, slowly at first, then with increasing tempo*)

THERE WAS A SUCKER
BORN EV'RY MINUTE
EACH TIME THE SECOND HAND SWEPT TO THE TOP

LIKE DANDELIONS UP THEY'D POP
THEIR EARS SO BIG, THEIR EYES SO WIDE
AND THOUGH I FED 'EM BONAFIDE
BALONEY
WITH NO TRUTH IN IT . . .

Blackout, and that's . . .

THE END